IAO

and the
Eurythmy Meditations

Werner Barfod

IAO

and the
Eurythmy Meditations

Published by the Section for the Arts of
Eurythmy, Speech, and Music of the School
of Spiritual Science, Goetheanum

MERCURY PRESS

Translated by Stephen Kicey
from the original German
IAO und die Eurythmischen Meditationen

Cover art and layout by Gabriela de Carvalho

Copyright © 1999 by Verlag am Goetheanum
This translation © 2001 by Mercury Press

ISBN 978-1-957569-54-3

MERCURY PRESS
an imprint of SteinerBooks
834 Main Street, PO Box 358
Spencertown, New York 12165
www.steinerbooks.org

|

Contents

Translator's Note

The eurythmist Werner Barfod, head of the Section for the Arts of Eurythmy, Speech and Music at the Goetheanum, is the author of several books on eurythmy, this one being the first to appear in English translation. His written work, with its terse style, will be familiar to the readers of the Section Newsletter, to which he regularly contributes.

In this book, Barfod presents a comprehensive outline of the "classical" meditative eurythmy exercises. These are practically described, oftentimes in Rudolf Steiner's own words. Related material from the Esoteric School and elements from the artistic renderings in the First Goetheanum help to place the exercises in a broader context. With its hands-on approach, the book addresses the active reader. It is like a workbook; one must try the exercises as one goes along.

As a further aid to approaching the deep wisdom of these exercises, Barfod draws attention to the results of his own personal research, for example differentiating the well-known eurythmy element of contraction and expansion into *"light-breathing"*, *"warmth-breathing"*, and *"life-breathing"* (see Chapters 9 and 10).

A few remarks regarding the translation itself may prove to be helpful. The text is extremely dense, even in the German original. Thus, it has been a real challenge attempting to make it accessible to the English reader while still remaining true to the intentions of the author, a difficulty often encountered with anthroposophic texts, and inherent to the current material. The reader is therefore strongly encouraged to enter into an active inner dialog with the author and the exercises presented. All translator's comments have been placed in [square brackets].

Following a usage familiar to eurythmists, the vowels retain their German values, and are denoted by italic capitals:

> *A* (*ah*), as in *father*
> *E* (*a*), as in *gate*
> *I* (*ee*), as in *meet*
> *O* (*oh*), as in *note*
> *U* (*oo*), as in *root*
> *Ue* (*eu*), as in *feud*

In order to avoid any confusion regarding the English personal pronoun "I", here used to represent the German term "*das ich*", it has been rendered as "the'I' (ego)", in contradistinction to the capitalized italic I, denoting the German vowel-sound (see above).

The German noun *Mensch* is a collective noun referring to both men and women. Having no direct English equivalent, it has been translated alternatively with "man" or "human being", depending on context. To avoid complications the personal pronoun "he" has generally been used in referring to it.

Without the support of others, this translation could not have been completed. I am indebted to Margaret Jonas of the Rudolf Steiner-House Library in London for her assistance with the endnotes, and to Maria ver Eecke, editor of the Eurythmy Association of North America Newsletter for her encouragement and many valuable suggestions for improving the text. To both of them my heartfelt thanks. In conclusion, I would particularly like to express my indebtedness and gratitude to Alan Stott, of Stourbridge, England, for his valuable assistance and encouragement at all stages of the work.

Stephen Kicey
December 2000

Introduction

Meditation is inner contemplation, an inner deepening, a way of spiritual concentration leading to self-knowledge. Within the anthroposophical context, meditation embraces paths of endeavor that enable the 'I' to work towards higher states of cognition.

With our day-waking consciousness we reflect the sense-perceptible world, forming mental pictures of this surrounding world. With our daytime-self, wakefully present within our body, we are capable of comprehending the world of concrete objects. At the other pole to the world of the senses there lies the spiritual world, which can only reveal itself to the human being who supersedes day-consciousness. Through meditation we can overcome the hindrances of the daytime-world that are present within our consciousness in order to be open for the spirit. If this succeeds, the spirit can draw near, and we can then take it up, each according to his or her abilities.

Just as, on the one hand we are cognitively connected with the world through the senses, on the other hand we are also linked to the world through our will, through our deeds. With the concepts and ideas gained from past experience, we are able to comprehend the world. By means of the motive for a deed we proceed from a future goal to the carrying out of the respective deed in the present. We use our present abilities to fulfill a task, the outcome of which lies in the future. Our cognitive thinking and trained will can both be further developed through meditation.

The processes of will involved in an action directed towards the world unfold within the unconscious realm. In meditative work it is a matter of liberating these will-processes from the world of solid, material objects. This means, to wake up in conscious, ensouled movements without reference to material objects – this we find in eurythmy. The eurythmy movements take their origin from spiritual-etheric movements which then become visible in soul-filled, expressive movements in the artistic process. Eurythmic meditation can be a means for a waking up to purely human movements, within which the awakened soul's essential nature can effectively reveal itself.

The human being encounters the spiritual world on two border thresholds: that of thinking and that of the will. The human being is centered within the body, wherein the 'I', as though breathed in, is open to the world. At the same time, too, the human being experiences that he is a being of the periphery, breathed out, as it were, with his 'I'. The goal is gradually to awaken, or rather to be able to maintain oneself in a state of heightened awareness, during the situation of sleep. For this, meditation is the means. Here shall be described only such eurythmy meditations that aim to illuminate the will with waking consciousness.

The process of artistic practice can also lead to a heightened awareness out of the active involvement itself; to a fashioning out of a tableau-consciousness, in a free and creative manner, at the moment of artistic presentation.

Werner Barfod
November 1998

I.
IAO

Chapter 1

The Path of the Soul through the Body to the Spirit: *IAO*

Introduction

The instrument of the 'I' (ego), through which evolutionary development takes place, is the earthly, upright human gestalt as fashioned by cosmic powers. The challenge is – and always has been – to seek the connecting link to the true 'I' through a concentration of the day-waking 'I', that is, a movement outwards from the midpoint to the circumference. This task is beautifully summarized in the verse on an old sundial:

> "Thou, O Man,
> utterance of God,
> be like the sun,
> at rest in the center of your movement." [1]

IAO in esoteric training

Man as a being of speech, of the Word, concentrates himself in the midst of the region of the heart on the movement suffusing his human form, his gestalt, with feeling. Long before the first beginnings of eurythmy, Rudolf Steiner had already given the *IAO*-exercise as a meditation. Later, *IAO* becomes the first gestalt-meditation in eurythmy, indeed, its very beginning and initial impulse. These two exercises are quite clearly related as metamorphoses of one and the same spiritual archetype.

We first meet the *IAO*-meditation in the material of the Esoteric School from 1904 to 1914:

13

"Mornings:
Concentrate on a line which passes
through the body:

The line does not pass through the spinal cord itself,
but rather through the body, somewhat *in front* of it." [2]

This, of course, is the *I* (*ee*) in the upright gestalt. Yet it is a quite
specific *I*, not to be conceived as identical with the spinal column,
but rather inside and lying before it. In the eurythmic *IAO*-exercise,
this column of light is actually felt to be even somewhat in front of
the gestalt. The eurythmic *I*, along with its arm-gesture, passes right
through the midst of the region of the heart.

With regard to the meditation, which is a gestalt-word meditation,
we read:

"Then meditate upon that which lies in the following words:
    Warming light [*] penetrates into me from above
    Weight of earth [*] spreads warmth-giving
    light within me and forms me.
Then, for a while, hold on to the thought:
    I am.
Then thinking of nothing; wait rather with an empty conscious
ness to see what comes." [3]

14

Here cosmic and earthly forces are addressed, just as in the eurythmy-meditation:

"I seek within me
the activity of creative forces,
the life of creative powers.
The earthly force of weight
speaks to me
through the word of my feet;
the forming might of the air
speaks to me
through the singing of my hands;
the power of heavenly light
speaks to me
through the thinking of my head,
how the world in the human being
speaks, sings, thinks."

[tr. Alan Stott]

("Ich suche im Innern
Der schaffenden Kräfte Wirken,
Der schaffenden Mächte Leben.
Es sagt mir
Der Erde Schweremacht
Durch meiner Füsse Wort,
Es sagt mir
Der Lüfte Formgewalt
Durch meiner Hände Singen,
Es sagt mir
Des Himmels Lichteskraft
Durch meines Hauptes Sinnen,
Wie die Welt im Menschen
Spricht, singt, sinnt.") [4]

"Warmth-giving light" and "the -power of heavenly light" penetrate
into the gestalt from above. "Weight of the earth" and "the earthly
forces of weight" stream through the gestalt from below, "and forms
me", as "the world in man speaks ...".

15

"Evenings:

Try to concentrate on your own bodily feelings, in the following stages:

> I am my head
> I am my throat
> I am my arms
> I am my enclosing chest.
> I am my heart
> I am the blood circulating within me
> I am my lungs

Then concentrate on your breathing in the following way:

Concentrate on the in-breathing, and experience the in-coming air as
> *I (ee).*

Concentrate on the air breathed-in as filling the body, and experience this air as
> *A (ah).*

Concentrate on the out-breathing, and experience the air leaving the body as
> *-O (oh).*

Do this for *seven* successive breathing-cycles; then concentrate in contemplation on the inside of the head. [Drawing: the point between the eyebrows and behind the forehead] Feel as though the word IAO sounds here; holding this sound for 1 – 2 minutes, then, thinking of *nothing*, await with an empty consciousness that which approaches."[5]

In the second part of the meditation, your attention is directed towards the upper and middle regions of the human being, and, in connection with in-breathing and out-breathing, towards *I, A* and *O*. This corresponds to "the forming might of the air" in the eurythmy-meditation, and so to the "circling round" of the circumference. We experience the in-breathed air more in our backs, as a bracing influence, and the out-breathing more in front of and around the chest.

16

The *A* and *O* of the eurythmy-exercise approximates to this quite closely, even though in the cited meditation a somewhat different level is being addressed, one that is entirely involved with the sphere of breathing.

In one variation of the *IAO*-meditation from the Esoteric School, the *I* is experienced only in the head. This corresponds to the raising of the head in the eurythmic *IAO*-exercise. *A* and *O* appear as a stream of light, more to the back or more to the front of the gestalt, respectively.

> "The stream of light from between the
> eyebrows to the nape of the neck: *I.*
> The stream of light runs along the spinal column: *A*.

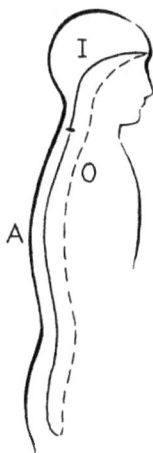

> The stream of light [flows] back within,
> from the spinal column back to the point
> between the eyebrows: *O*."

[Repeat the above] seven times, 2 minutes each (= 14 minutes).
>   *"IAO* penetrates into me, through me, out of me.
>   *IAO* engenders forces within me, through me, out of me.
>   *IAO* lives weaving in me, through me, out of me."

Repeat as often (as) possible.

> *"pervading mood:*
> *IAO* as the name of Christ.
> This is connected to the secret of how Christ
> works in the human being." [6]

Here *IAO* is clearly bound up with the name of Christ and with the mystery of His working within the human being. *IAO* as a triad, "in me – through me – out of me", throws light on how the *I* penetrates into me, how the *A* streams through me, and how the *O* proceeds from me. The very same qualities are also the basis of the first exercise in eurythmy, the *IAO*. It is the seminal exercise of the whole of eurythmy.

Chapter 2

J and *B* – the Pillars of Wisdom and of Life – and the *IAO*-Meditation in a Variety of Forms

In lecture one of the speech-eurythmy lecture-course, Steiner speaks of the Logos, the creative power of the Word, which once embraced "the entire human being as an etheric creation". "When someone speaks, we are dealing with a human creation, with an etheric human creation." The etheric body is the wisdom of the human being. "In speaking, something exceptionally significant occurs. The human being assumes form. And we can give a fairly complete picture of man's soul-life, by portraying all-embracing feelings. *IAO*, representing so much of soul-life, represents almost the whole content of the human soul in its aspect of feeling: *IAO*." [7]

During the Theosophical Convention in Munich, at Pentecost 1907, Steiner decorated the hall with apocalyptic seals, planetary columns and planetary forms. He also placed two pillars into the space – a red pillar called Jachin, and a blue pillar called Boaz. The pillars stand for wisdom and strength, as the foundation for human life. At one time they were the Tree of Life and the Tree of Knowledge. With the appearance of birth and death, man paid dearly for his knowledge. The deeper meaning is expressed in the words: "I am the one who was; I am the one who is; I am the one who will be." [8]

These pillars confront mankind today as one-sided tasks. Man has to learn to maintain his balance while passing between them, because only in the balanced state between the two is life to be found. The third 'pillar', the rainbow uniting both, embodies the principle of devotion – of love and beauty. The connection is to be found through Christ, through a love cleansed and purified. [9]

Steiner aphoristically unites the occult wisdom of the two pillars in verse-form (lecture, 21st May, 1907):

19

The red pillar:

> "In pure thought you find
> the self which endures.
> Transform thought into image
> and you experience creative wisdom."

The blue pillar:

> "Intensify feeling into light
> and you reveal formative power.
> Consolidate the will to being
> and you actively create in world-existence."

> *("Im reinen Gedanken findest du*
> *Das Selbst, das sich halten kann.*
> *Wandelst zum Bilde du den Gedanken,*
> *Dann erlebst du die schaffende Weisheit.*
>
> *Verdichtest du das Gefühl zum Licht,*
> *Dann offenbarst du die formende Kraft.*
> *Verdinglichst du den Willen zum Wesen,*
> *So schaffest du im Weltensein.")* [10]

Here the magical power lies in the transition from the verse of the first pillar to the verse of the second.

Within this feeling of balanced harmony permeating the soul's entire being, *AIO* sounds.

- the human being, full of wonder and self-amazement, experiencing creative wisdom within his own being: *A (ah)*
- the human being standing upright in the world, laying hold at the same time of both midpoint and periphery in harmonious balance: *I (ee)*
- the human being revealed as a being of soul through active sympathy, as a shaping force within world-existence: *O (oh)*.

In passing between these pillars, the human being experiences the archetypal sounding of *AIO* out of the pillars' wisdom. In an even more comprehensive manner than in the speech-eurythmy lecture-course, or so it would seem, there sounds forth within *AIO* the life of soul as a totality, as thinking, feeling and will.

The following meditation from an esoteric lesson directly relates to this, having once again the three main vowels as its content:

> "*OAIAO:* the 'I' (ego) in the midst of light and space
> *AIOIA:* space for the 'I' and for the light
> *IOAOI:* light through space and through myself
> I am."[11]

The sequence of the main speech-sounds, *IAO*, manifests here in a variety of ways, yet always mirrored symmetrically around a center.

Each of the three sounds is flanked respectively by the other two, revealing certain qualitative relationships:

I with the 'I' (ego)	Each *IAO*-sequence corresponds to a different level:
A with light	cosmic – historical – earthly
O with space	–
	of the soul – gestalt-orientated, and so on.
	(We shall return to this later.)

Another indication found in the notes of the Esoteric School, points to the relationship of the hierarchies to the vowels of the same esoteric lesson:

> "*IAO* Seraphim, Cherubim and, in part, Thrones are involved
> *U* Kyriotetes, Exusiai, Dynamis
> *E* Archai, Archangeloi, Angeloi."[12]

These correspondences act as a direct link to the painted artistic rendering in the great cupola of the First Goetheanum in the threefold

IAO-motif above the proscenium arch. The following indications given as a preparation to a meditation also seem to be a direct transition:

> "*I* – still within yourself.
> *A* – you open yourself to the world, which has much to say.
> *O* – the angels come, reaching out to join hands in greeting.
> *U* – the second hierarchy follows, flooding you with light.
> *E* – the first hierarchy comes and consumes you in fire." [13]

The theme of the pillars sounds once again in the fourth apocalyptic seal, the one pillar resting within the water's stream of life, the other standing solidly upon a firmly-built, earthly foundation. The pillar-motif also appears within the *O*-motif, as depicted in the great cupola of the First Goetheanum. In the next chapter this will be gone into in more detail. It is a mystery of humanity, bound up with the Being of the Sun, Christ, and which accompanies the whole stream of earthly becoming, as does the *IAO*.

Chapter 3

The Threefold *IAO*-motif in the Great Cupola of the First Goetheanum

In the great cupola, to the east, immediately above the proscenium arch, there stands a threefold motif which Steiner called *IAO*. In sublime imagery there appears the cosmic representation [cosmically rendered image] of the human being. [Through sublime imagery the macrocosmic form of the human being is revealed.]

"And finally, the results of lemurian and atlantean evolutionary development are portrayed. What our present era is meant to be, is represented through the fact that when you direct your gaze from the west to the east, towards the smaller space, there approaches the impulse that lies within world-becoming that declares itself in *IAO*, through the way the imagery has been made. It is not that *IAO* appears in some merely symbolic form, but it is expressed through the motif. Directing your gaze from the east to the west corresponds to what speaks out of the depths of the cosmos into cultural evolution, just as the *IAO* speaks from within into the soul's evolution." [14]

The three motifs depict the human being as cosmic man in his primordial threefold being, in the vertical axis from above downwards:

The "head-man", painted out of a strong, energetic red, "God's Wrath and God's Sorrow", characterized as *I (ee)*.

A yellow-red pillar of fire strives upwards, proceeding from a blue terrestrial globe held in God's hands. A dark ahrimanic being grasps after the divine light. Mighty divine eyes observe the struggle between light and darkness. Angelic beings flood the pillar of fire with light, within which the human being actively builds upon his own 'I' (ego).

Underneath the head-motif there is a triangle with seven luminous figures of light, the basis of the "middle man": "The Dance of the Seven", characterized as *A*. The beings, in radiant yellow, pass each other as in a circle-dance. The triangle, opening downwards, is surrounded by violet; a red countenance is shown within. In the rhythmical swinging and swaying of the three-plus-four beings between inside and outside, the heart takes form in the center.

Below the central motif of the Seven, there appears "The Circle of the Twelve", surrounded by "divine arms" within a background the color of peach-blossom. At the same time, the twelve countenances show the foundations for the human senses. "The Circle of the Twelve" is characterized as *O*. To the left, a divine hand points downwards, indicating rugged black cliffs. Seven of the countenances have a light background; five are in darker surroundings, completely in accord with the distribution of color in the zodiac. Seven blue angelic beings are assisting from above. Down below upon the earth, two pillars are standing, supporting two of the countenances. The gesture of the *O* embraces the forces of the will, the depths of fate; it embraces birth and death, arrival on the earth, and departure from it.

Steiner once characterized this trinity of motifs in the following manner:
"What you see in the great cupola to the east, is a kind of impression, a feeling of your own 'I' (ego). This 'I' is a kind of trinity, if one may use this word. It is revealed inwardly, too, ranging on the one hand as far as the light-filled clarity and transparency of the thinking-'I', and on the other hand, the other pole, delving into the will, the 'I' of will, and in the middle moving towards the feeling-'I'." [15]

We find Steiner's drawings and sketches, along with detailed descriptions, in Hilde Raske, *The Language of Color in the First Goetheanum* (Walter Keller Verlag, Dornach 1987). [16]

*IAO in Rudolf Steiner's rough sketch of a stage-curtain
for eurythmy performances*

The curtain was to hang in the First Goetheanum, directly beneath the threefold motif in the great dome as a kind of continuation, composed of three horizontally-ordered motifs, from left to right: Earthly Man – *IAO*. These two representations (the vertical and the horizontal) can be experienced as the two beams of a processual cross [two processes coinciding in a particular, mutually shared phase, the "crossing-point"], with the *A* as the central heart. The sketch depicts three portal-like motifs standing adjacent to each other.

To the left is a portal, held in warm, brown tones. An upwardly-striving flame surrounded by warm red and orange hues rises above. Weight has been overcome through the strength of the upright, the gestalt appears as the *I (ee)*.

The middle portal opens into light-yellow surroundings, bounded by a delicate blue that arches above. Two angelic beings in reddish tones are inclining downwards, hovering over a pale orange triangle, their open arms outstretched. A freely-breathing flow and a streaming movement are evident; a breathing rhythm sets in; a bright, light-filled *A* can be experienced.

The third portal towers high above the other two, all in blue within an enclosing arch, receptive to the blue surroundings. Blue angelic beings hover within the arches' curving vault with *O*-like gestures. The in-streaming forces are internalized, are made one's own.

Passing from warm, reddish-brown tones, through shades of orange, and ending in a delicate blue, the curtain motifs flow above the portals, forming themselves as a whole. In this way with see in visual imagery the human being, in *IAO*.

When the curtain opens, eurythmists appear upon the stage. Through and on each individual gestalt, movements become visible. As soul-filled movements, they follow spiritual-etheric laws through which weight appears to have been overcome. These moving human forms are like pictures, through which the eurythmy strives to shine forth. And man as a being of soul and spirit can himself be revealed as the one who is active, speaking and singing in eurythmy. It is the task of both eurythmists and audience today to make the "curtain" transparent, in order to learn to behold the mystery of the human being. [17]

Chapter 4

IAO –
the First Eurythmic Exercise

The first eurythmy gestalt and speech-sound exercise, *IAO*, was given by Rudolf Steiner early in September 1912, in Munich:

"Stand upright and try to experience a column, whose base is the balls of your feet, and whose capital is your own head, your forehead. And this column, this uprightness, learn to experience it as *I (ee)* "[18]

We have already pointed out that this upright experience does not coincide with the upright of the physical gestalt. Only through an additional activity can it be experienced as a column of light extending between the balls of the feet, the breastbone, and the forehead. This column of light vibrates in harmony with the meridian of feeling uniting the main chakras. (The meridian of feeling runs vertically, just to the front of the gestalt; the meridian of the will is behind the gestalt.) The vertical impulse within the column of light is experienced as *I,* that *I* which makes possible the connection between my everyday sense of self and my own higher being.

"Now shift the head of the column so that it is behind the base, and that you will learn to perceive as *A (ah)*."[19]

Here it is essential that your awareness of the column of light does not disappear. When tilting backward, sustain the feeling of the *I*-sound, keeping within it and thereby intensifying the 'back space', the plane of the will along your back and a feeling of strength directed towards the earth. There emerges a feeling of *A (ah)*, originating in and proceeding from the human gestalt, open to the earth.

"Tilt the head of the column so that it is in front of the base, and learn to perceive that as *O (oh)*." [20]

We take once again the upright axis of the column of light with us while moving into the forward space, maintaining ourselves in the feeling of *I*, experiencing our immersion in the world before us, without falling into it. On the level of feeling we experience the *O*, precisely because of the restraint exercised in our own gestalt. In a felt communion with the world's being in the periphery, there lives the strength of devotion.

The Relationship of the IAO-exercise to the Chakras

Already in this seminal exercise, eurythmy reveals itself to be a well-spring of the spirit manifesting on the human being. Through the meridian of feeling, the chakra-meridian, the whole gestalt is sensitized, emotionally activated, in its etheric totality. Although all the chakras are addressed, three of them are involved directly:

The root-chakra, the four-petalled lotus-flower, rays right down to the feet of the human being who is standing. The ten-petalled lotus-flower, the solar plexus, works here in conjunction with the root-chakra. The column of light touches the heart chakra, the twelve-petalled lotus-flower, via the breastbone. The forehead, with the two-petalled lotus-flower, forms the capital, the topmost point of the column of light. It is precisely because the column of light is maintained, moving together with the upright gestalt, that the meridian of feeling remains activated throughout the whole exercise.

The etheric body as a self-contained whole enclosing the bodily gestalt, is activated on a soul-level by the sounds bound up with the gestalt. An etheric breathing process can be inwardly experienced. Within the etheric body, the lotus-flowers are organs of life; within the soul they are the seeds of spiritual organs of perception. By means of the chakras here mentioned the human being unites himself, as in the meditation for eurythmists, with the earth through his feet, with the surroundings through his chest, and with the light, the heavens, through his head.

This light-axis, here developed through practicing the I, the strength of the upright as an etheric column of light, is the basic prerequisite of all eurythmic activity.

The IAO-meditation and Wonder, Compassion, and Conscience

The three sounds of the *IAO*-exercise are the three main vowels, and are at the same time the vowels that embody the soul-forces. Eurythmy is the art which manifests on the human instrument, and through which the supersensible realm, the spirit, can be directly experienced within the sense-perceptible realm. Eurythmy by its very nature, is an art of the threshold.

The earthly human being opens his soul to the starry heavens, full of trust. This, then, is an indication of his cosmic origins. In someone who is full of astonishment and wonder we see man wishing to free himself of his bodily sheaths, wishing to become one with the world, in this way revealing his spiritual origins.

"It is as though something of a spiritual nature would penetrate into us, come into relation with our own soul-nature, and then actually cleave us in two." This is the power of *A*, which unites the human being with "his two stars". From this vantage point, he experiences himself in wonder as a human being incarnated in a physical body. [21]

The feeling of compassion, of sympathy and devotion, impels a person to go beyond his own personal limits and concerns, to enter into the sphere of another being. It ultimately leads him into communion with all creation.

"We face something spiritual, that is capable of declaring itself to us, that through its own being communicates something to us." This is the power of *O*, the power with which man unites himself with all

29

the beings of the world. [22] Together with the power of the upright between the earth and the heavens, light penetrates into the human being from above. And at the same time, through this light, the voice of conscience is awakened within us. Thanks to his conscience, the human being matures, growing beyond the bounds of his bodily nature and into the spirit. The voice of conscience acts as a corrective upon human behavior. Through the sound *I (ee)* man identifies himself with his own true self. We possess "the consolidation of our spiritual being within ourselves." [23] As a being endowed with selfhood, incarnated in a body upon the earth, man is able to express astonishment and compassion, and can hear the voice of conscience.

In the course of mankind's development, these forces are taken hold of in succession. With the appearance of Christ on earth, in particular through his death and resurrection, it became possible for the human being to internalize these three forces and make them his own.

The Christ-Impulse remains united with the soul. At the end of earthly evolution, the human being will have attained his completion and fullest unfolding, and will be in harmony with the Christ-Impulse. Astonishment and wonder, these ultimately stream towards the Christ, and assist in forming the astral body for the Christ-Impulse. And everything that can lay hold of human souls as love and compassion forms the etheric body of the Christ-Impulse. And what lives as conscience in human beings, ensouling them, from the Mystery of Golgotha until the attainment of the earth's ultimate goal, forms the physical body – or rather, that which corresponds to it – for the Christ-Impulse.[24]

It is worth remarking that both *IAO* as the first eurythmic exercise and meditation given by Steiner to eurythmists, and the *TAO* – given 1924 in the music-eurythmy lecture-cycle [25] as a eurythmy gestalt-meditation – correspond both in structure and in the sequence of the speech-sounds to the three forces of wonder, love and conscience.

Chapter 5

The Seven Stages of Metamorphosis
of the *IAO*-Exercise

The *IAO-meditation*, in which the human being experiences himself as a being of the Word, placed into the region between heaven and earth with his bodily gestalt, has been discussed in detail. It is the seminal exercise for a series of *IAO*-metamorphoses in eurythmy, beginning with the gestalt-exercise and unfolding into realms of soul and spirit within the course of time and beyond, as far as the realities of cosmic being, the divine.

The *second stage* is the *IAO*-exercise whose content is the threefold gestalt as the dwelling of the soul. With the I we raise ourselves into the upright, particularly experiencing the light-filled upper part of the body and the head. A jump into a powerful, broadly-open *A* with the legs comes next. Then the arms form a balance to these two poles with the *O* at the level of the heart. The gestalt remains still for a moment like a sounding chord before its arpeggiated release in the reverse order: first the *O*-gesture is released, then the *A*-jump, and finally, the head relaxes. The exercise is then repeated several times, always in the same unchanging order of build-up and release. Thereafter, the tempo is first increased and then decreased again. It is an exercise which assists the process of incarnation, promoting harmony of the soul within the body, and is consequently often used in education and therapy. [26]

In the *third stage* the soul enters into relation with the world. *I, A* and *O*, as the primary soul-sounds, appear in the zones and form-movements in space corresponding to thinking – feeling – will. The soul, using the gestalt as its instrument, faces the world in these functions.

In thinking, perception of the world is prerequisite. The perceptions are then related one to the other, resulting in the development of concepts. The *A* in the zone of thinking in front of the heart, with the head and hands brought into relationship, is the eurythmy gesture for thinking. It is only with the heart that we are capable of understanding. [27] The corresponding spatial forms consist of straight paths leading from me to some object, then to a different object, and so on, finally returning to me as the one who understands.

In feeling, the soul breathes out its own being into the world and then returns to itself in continuous alternation. When the prevailing mood is one of joy, then the feeling-filled *I* stretches itself, reaching upwards, shining brightly. And when mourning presses upon the soul, the *I* sinks downwards in sorrow. The gaze accompanies the movement of the *I,* turning lightly and brightly upwards, or following it downwards, subdued. In the spatial forms, straight elements are intermingled with curved ones; here, too, there is a breathing out and a flowing back again to the self.

In the will, the soul steps actively and effectively into the world. Strongly formed and invested with self-control, the arms lay hold of the *O* below, in the zone of the will. The clear and open gaze is directed outwards. The will expresses itself spatially in ceaselessly curving, twisting form-movements, the polar opposite of thinking.

The dionysian quality of the soul has been discussed here only with regard to the sounds *I, A* and *O*. A complete description of all that is otherwise entailed lies outside the scope of the present study.

We have come to see man as a being of the Word here on the Earth. We then learned to view the soul's own internal organization in connection with the gestalt. And in the third stage we have experienced the soul's relation to the world as a further degree of metamorphosis. In the *fourth stage*, man as a being of soul and spirit enters into relation with the threefold revelation of time. You stand entirely in the present, your arms spread wide horizontally in front of you. Fully awake, the *I (ee)* in the gestalt and the gesture stretches to the horizon, in this way sustaining itself at the crossing point. [28]

You dive into the past, eurythmically, drawing yourself together in the gestalt, sinking downwards towards the earth. At the same time you remain as upright as possible, with the arms in *A*, open to the earth, receiving that which was.

The gestalt is stretched, striving towards the future, seeming to pull itself apart. You rise on to the very tips of your toes, the whole force of the will directed towards the future. The arms reach upwards, above the head, embracing the approaching time-stream with the *O*-gesture – or else reaching out to meet it with *U*.

In the *fifth stage* of the *IAO*-metamorphosis, we pass through the cultural epochs, following the course of mankind's journey through the ages. Here the soul and spiritual being progresses through the incarnations, experiencing the three primary speech sounds with ever-new levels of consciousness.

For the *third cultural epoch*, the experiencing of *JOA* within the approaching light-ether body still formed a part of the content of the Mysteries.

"This *JOA*, that [the initiate] knew, would enliven his 'I' (ego) and his astral body. *JO* is 'I' and astral body, and the approach of the light-ether body is *A – JOA*. Then, because of the *JOA* vibrating within him, he felt he was 'I', astral body, and etheric body. And then it was as though there would sound upwards from the earth – for the human being had been displaced into the cosmos – there would sound upwards from the earth that which the *JOA* then interfused: *eh-v*. These were the forces of the earth, rising up in the *eh-v*.

$$J_{eh}O_vA$$

And now, in the *JehOvA* he felt the human being in his totality." [29] From out of the realm of pre-earthly existence, the human being feels his own essence drawing near, and also feels that which fills the body, gently consonantal in nature, arising towards him from the earth.

In the *fourth cultural epoch*, we arrive at the Mystery of Golgotha, poised between the Greek and Roman cultures. The Son of God, Christ, the Being of the Sun unites himself with his body, with the Earth. Out of *JOA* there arises *AIO* – the Christ enters into the human earthly sphere, as cosmic Logos.

> "I am the Alpha and the Omega
> thus speaks the Lord, our God,
> which is, and which was, and which is to come,
> the Lord of the Universe." [30]

With the *fifth cultural epoch*, we arrive at our present age. Out of the light of anthroposophy, out of the situation of the consciousness-soul, the individual human being emerges with the *IAO*, with the task of turning to meet the cosmos. *IAO* becomes a meditation on the path of self-development, as described at the beginning of these studies; *IAO* becomes a eurythmy meditation.

In accord with these three cultural epochs, the metamorphosis proceeds, as it were, through the Trinity, from the Father-God to the Son-God to the Spirit-God, from *JOA* to *AIO* to *IAO*. In the course of future epochs it will transform itself still further, no doubt also appearing in the reversed order; the final metamorphosis coinciding with the *TAO*.

In the *sixth stage* of the *IAO*-metamorphosis we enter in our present age upon the spiritual level of the objective "It" *("Es")*.
The main exercise of the inner schooling, and the accompanying "six basic exercises" unite the human soul-forces with the forces of the cosmos: "I am – It thinks – She feels – He wills."
It thinks: the World-Thinking. – She feels: the World-Soul. – He wills: the Cosmic-Will. [31]
The sounds *I, A, O* are also associated with these soul-forces: Thinking – *A,* Feeling – *I,* Will – *O,* along with the corresponding soul-related zones: Thinking – middle, Feeling – above, Will – below.

34

Through the objectifying transformation of thinking into Cosmic Thinking, the zone changes, shifting upwards from the middle to the upper one, the zone of truth, receptively open with *A*.

Through the objectifying transformation of feeling to Cosmic Feeling, the zone changes, shifting downwards from the upper to the middle one, with *I*. The *I* becomes objective feeling in the periphery, receptive and open. The greatest expression of love is *I* in the zone of *A*. It is the zone of beauty.

Through the objectifying transformation of will to Cosmic Will, the lower zone remains unchanged, with *O*. The Cosmic Will forms out of the periphery, however, just as the personal will proceeds from the center. It is the zone of goodness.

And so, through the objectifying process, and by identifying the sounds with thinking – feeling – will, *IAO* receives a set of newly transformed zones that as a result are capable of expressing spiritual qualities. In working eurythmically with Rudolf Steiner's mantric language this is absolutely essential.

In the seventh stage of the *IAO*-metamorphosis, the cycle is completed. Man as a being of the Word unites himself with the cosmos and with the Trinity, as expressed in Steiner's Foundation Stone Verse. [32]

The first part of the Foundation Stone Verse begins with the limbs, with the region of the will, within which the eurythmy, too, comes to expression. This region is determined, however, by the Father-God: "For the Father Spirit of the heights holds sway / In Depths of Worlds begetting Being." The first hierarchy, the Spirits of Strength – "Let out of the heights ring forth / What in depths below finds echo" – affirm the zone of action. This hierarchy works through the human being from the heights into the depths, out of the cosmos down upon the earth.

And suddenly, it is *A* that appears in the lower zone, becoming the sound which takes in the divine-fatherly forces.

The second part of the Foundation Stone Verse begins with the "beat of heart and lung", the region of feeling, which is determined and objectified by the periphery, and thus appears in the middle zone when carried out eurythmically. This region is determined by the Son-God, Christ: "For the Christ-Will in the encircling round holds sway / In the rhythms of worlds, bestowing grace on the Soul." The second hierarchy, the Spirits of Light – "Let there be fired from the East / What through the West is formed" – emphasize the mighty activity in the periphery. This hierarchy works from cosmic expanses, peripherally, through the human being.

The *I* in the middle zone becomes a freely breathing exchange with the periphery, and a eurythmically balancing movement: the strength of Christ, freely penetrating the human being in a selfless *I (ee)*.

The third part of the Foundation Stone Verse begins with the resting head, with the region of thought, which receives the cosmic thoughts through cosmic light. Thus, thinking, too, is objectified, and cosmically open; eurythmically speaking, it resides in the upper zone. The region is determined by the Spirit-God, who reigns in the cosmic thoughts, actively working "In the World-Being, imploring light". The third hierarchy, the Spirits of Soul – "Let there be asked from the depths, what in the heights is answered" – determine the zone of action. This hierarchy is active from the depths to the heights, working with the help of the angels through the human being right into the cosmos.

Here resounds the expressive power of *O*, filled with living spirit; the eurythmy is performed in the upper zone, where the divine-spiritual is at work.

Thus, again at this level, an interchange occurs between *O* and *A*, between will and thinking. On this highest, objectified level the human being is united once more with his divine origin.

It must also be mentioned that the sounds *IAO* are eurythmically present throughout the whole of the Foundation Stone Verse. Already at the very start, in the silent prelude, the speech-sounds are *IAO*, and in fact in contrapuntal interplay between the middle figure and the five in the periphery. They are contrapuntal both in the sequence of the speech-sounds *IAO – OAI* and in the three zones: above – middle – below. This has a tremendously stimulating effect between below and above, and above and below, respectively; and in the middle zone all are in accord. Consequently, it should not be at all surprising when the "Human Soul" is actually directly addressed! And during the fourth part, "the turning-point of time", the first Christmas, those standing and listening to the text perform *IAO* several times, in the zones that correspond to the text.

Chapter 6

IAO as Exercise of Balance –
Portraying the Luciferic and Ahrimanic Beings

One particularly characteristic feature of *IAO* as seminal exercise and eurythmy meditation is, that, by means of the column of light present in the *I* and maintained throughout all three phases of the exercise, the doer is centered and actively involved with his or her whole being. While leaning back into the *A*, and while inclining forwards in *O,* he feels himself held, supported by the column of light. Now, it is a characteristic of the adversaries that, in their undying vigil, they immediately intervene, setting to work the moment something falls out of our sense of inner balance. A moment of inattention or carelessness during the course of an activity, of whatever kind, immediately calls forth one or both of them on to the field of action.

The great value of the *IAO*-exercise becomes apparent once more, when it is deliberately employed as a means of forming an experiential basis for the depiction of the luciferic and ahrimanic beings.

We position ourselves within the column of light of the *I*, lean back into the *A*, supported, carried by this column of light; and then we release it, suddenly. We feel ourselves helplessly abandoned to the leaning slant of *A*, and fall backwards. Only by taking quickly-placed steps are we able to avoid falling over in fact. This falling into weight in *A* is precisely the first movement-experience needed in portraying the ahrimanic beings. Moving as though directed from without, we seize hold of our bodily instrument, mastering the heaviness. And we move with the *A* downwards, the gesture bent, "broken" at the elbows. This delineates the fundamental experience that can be acquired by working with the *IAO*-exercise; the further steps needed in the portrayal of these beings will not be pursued here.

Positioning ourselves once more within the *I*-column, we then lean forward into the *O*, again maintaining our upright through the column of light, and experiencing as intensively as possible the filled, rounded *O*-space before us. And then suddenly, letting go of the column of light, we feel we are being absorbed, sucked up into the *O*-space. We will have to repeat this several times before we succeed in falling forwards and yet not allowing ourselves to be drawn down into weight and heaviness. The effects of weight are suspended in the *O*-space, even though they naturally continue to be active physically. This feeling of being absorbed, taken up by the *O*-space is exactly the initial experience needed for developing a portrayal of the luciferic beings. Here, too, we take hold of our instrument as though guided from without, and together with the dwindling *I*-force we are sucked into the *O*. The bent, "broken" gesture of *I* within the *O*-space is the gesture of Lucifer. By allowing oneself to be inspired by a bright red both in the movement and in the periphery, the gesture is intensified. Grey has a similar effect with respect to Ahriman, regarding the hard, coldly-objective appearance of the bent *A*-gesture.

This all applies primarily to the development and portrayal of the gestalt as it is sucked up into the light, or as it falls into weight, with the corresponding "broken" gestures. The stepping [manner of walking], spatial forms, colors, finger positions, and the way movements are formed can all be evolved out of the basic elements by pursuing an analogous process.

Chapter 7

TAO as a Source and Eurythmic Meditation as a Challenge for the Future

TAO is probably the oldest mystery-word known to mankind. It is part of our atlantean heritage, and since that time it has provided the connecting link to the gods. It will continue accompanying us till far into the future.

In the lecture from 16th November, 1905 (in GA 54), Steiner speaks about the human being's connection to the gods of the actively creative past, present and future with regard to the *TAO*:

"For a large portion of mankind, *TAO* expresses – as for the greater part of humanity already for millennia it has expressed – the highest to which humanity could aspire, and of which humanity thought that the world, the whole of humanity, will one day aspire. It is the highest that the human being carries as a seed, which one day will blossom fully out of innermost human nature. *TAO* signifies both a deep, hidden fundament of the soul and an exalted future." [33]

In February of 1924, during the music-eurythmy lecture-cycle, Steiner gives the *TAO*-exercise, calling it an "esoteric interlude", a "eurythmic meditation".[34] He describes in detail what is needed in preparation actually to do the meditation: the note/interval sequence, the movement in time – starting with a short and ending with a sustained sound – and also the corresponding speech-sounds. The notes B/A are to sound together, then, in closing, E and D are allowed to sound on. As keynote-related intervals [degrees of the scale] we have: seventh/sixth, then third and second (sustained). In the tonal–vowel correspondence, the musical seventh/sixth corresponds to *I/Ue* , the third corresponds to *A*, and the second corresponds to *O*. Then, in place of *I/Ue*, the *T* appears. Out of the soul's response, there arises the cosmic impact coming from Leo: *T*.

40

There occurs here a metamorphosis of the *IAO*-exercise into the *TAO*. Again, it is primarily the phonetic aspect which is of interest. All else is described only to the extent necessary in this context. In Steiner's description it remains open as to how the meditation itself is actually to be done, even though traditionally its seems natural first to perform the interval-gestures to the sequence of musical sounds as they are played, and then to follow up with the corresponding speech-sounds (phonetic correspondences) as *TAO*. It is characteristic that, as with all eurythmy meditations, it is carried out in standing. Steiner calls *TAO* "a wonderful means of making your inner bodily nature flexible, inwardly supple, and able to be artistically fashioned for eurythmy."[35]

What follows is an attempt to describe in outline one possible form for practicing *TAO* as a meditative exercise. We begin with its cosmic source, the zodiacal gesture for *Leo*. The *T* is then performed as the soul's response, "meaningfully streaming forces from above downwards", "striking powerfully, like a bolt of lightning."[36] Afterwards, like an awakening of the soul, musically, the seventh/sixth sounds together with the corresponding eurythmy interval-gestures. These are followed by the E/third note/interval-gestures and the corresponding speech-sound gesture of *A*, concluding with the sustained D/second note and interval gestures, and the corresponding *O*-gesture. The whole series of events thus merges together into a single, unified process, that "makes you inwardly flexible". Both the note and interval gestures and the speech-sounds are laid hold of inwardly, becoming thereby a unified whole within the movement-flow.

As already described in connection with *IAO*, the forces of conscience, wonder and compassion, as forces of the Christ-Impulse, can be experienced inwardly within the meditation when carried out in this integrated manner. In this context the *T*-impulse actively becomes the awakening herald of conscience, to which the two-note chord imparts musical expressiveness. Raising oneself into the upright, and turning towards the cosmos with the zodiacal gesture, the impulse of conscience is taken up and affirmed. There now follows, with the musical third and the soul's response from the center, from the heart, the unfolding of *A*, wonder; and with the musical second the soul responds in loving union with the *O*.

With this meditation, the doer places himself or herself in connection with his or her spiritual origin, from out the well-springs of eurythmy and anthroposophy. Here lies one of man's tasks within the culture of the present and of future ages. This is a universally human impulse, to which eurythmy has an essential contribution to make.

II.

The Eurythmy Meditations

Chapter 8

The Eurythmy Meditations

We know of seven eurythmy meditations, although Rudolf Steiner apparently uses the expression only in connection with "I think speech" and *TAO*. All these exercises share the primary characteristic of being carried out in standing. In each, our attention is directed to a sequence of movements which on the one hand is gestalt-related, and which on the other hand enlarges the soul, bringing it into relation with a cosmic periphery. Nearly all the eurythmy meditations connect gestalt-geometry with a sequence of speech-sounds demanding active ensoulment, or alternatively with an accompanying text or a single word. The "archetypal color-gestures" as meditation occupy the midpoint in this series of seven exercises carried out on the upright human being. Here an ethical strength of soul is called upon, in order to fill the gestures with a color-experience.

Alongside the exercise "We seek the soul – we are illumined by the spirit" *("Wir suchen die Seele – Uns strahlet der Geist")* Rudolf Steiner writes "*Vita eurythmo-Geometrie*" as an exclamation of enthusiasm. [37] Strictly speaking, this exercise is not a meditation. Yet, it is precisely this working together of Euclidean geometry (the spiral determined by the midpoint working radially towards the periphery) and projective geometry (the spiral determined as tangential envelope-curve out of the periphery) which make *eurythmic* geometry possible. This applies to all the eurythmy meditations, with their intrinsic gestalt-geometry.

In all of these meditations it is a matter of employing inner concentration and a feeling for the gestalt in order to make the etheric body supple, sensitizing it for the movement-instrument, awakening the energy-centers and uniting the person who is practicing with the light-ether, warmth-ether, chemical ether and life-ether. Each exercise focuses on one or more qualities which can be brought to experience through concrete practice. Nevertheless, it is only via our feelings, that is, indirectly, that we can become consciously aware of the etheric realm.

The *first eurythmy meditation* is indeed the first in all respects, both in the historical development of eurythmy and in the meditative sequence. It enables the experiencing of the etheric body in its self-contained wholeness:

IAO.

It is the feeling-soul's pathway to the spirit, through the gestalt! The gestalt really stands at the center of this exercise, the arms remaining at rest on the gestalt. The crucial thing is the human being raising himself into the upright position. Standing upon the earth, he unites himself with the light from above. Maintaining the *I (ee)*-pillar before the gestalt is probably the most important aspect. Your attention is directed towards the ball of the foot, the breastbone and the forehead. This is where the meridian of feeling connected with the chakras runs. Through the solar plexus (ten-petalled lotus flower), together with the root-chakra (four-petalled lotus flower), we overcome earthly heaviness; the heart-chakra (twelve-petalled lotus flower) is touched; and the forehead (two-petalled lotus flower) forms the capital of the pillar of light, within which the practitioner is as one with the light.

The etheric body as enveloping sheath around the gestalt is activated; the instrument is tuned. The pause after the exercise, in which the upright posture is relaxed, aids the imprinting of the activated impulses within the gestalt, and the closing of the energy-centers. Because the exercise has already been described in detail, here we simply point to the meditative source.

The *second eurythmy meditation* derives from esoteric mystery-traditions, as does the IAO-exercise. Rudolf Steiner describes it in a lecture in *Rosicrucianism and Modern Initiation*:

"Light streams upwards,
Weight bears downwards."

*("Licht strömt aufwärts,
Schwere lastet abwärts.")*

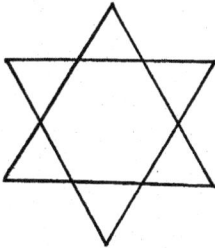

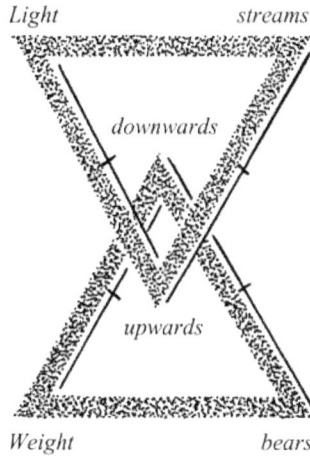

This exercise became in eurythmy a gestalt-exercise in which, through the polarities of light and weight, there arises an open, free space in the middle of the gestalt that acts as the source of all human movement. The upwardly-striving triangle, arising out of the middle region of the gestalt, is formed with the arms stretched upwards and is filled with the soul-content – "Light streams upwards". This content has to be actively willed from the region of the heart. Then, from the middle of the gestalt downwards, the other triangle is formed with the legs, through which the body's weight bears upon the earth – "Weight bears downwards." When both triangles are formed by the gestalt at the same time, in perfect lateral symmetry and with the accompanying soul-content, this free space becomes discernible as a feeling around the solar plexus – it is the well-spring for all movement. The uniting of the gestalt with the earth and the cosmos is similar to that of the first meditation, and yet by experiencing the gestalt in its opposing polarities something completely different occurs. The body is endowed with the source of life. In the middle, poised between light and weight, warmth arises, filled with the living spirit which can take hold of the gestalt. Two levels

47

(which are not polarities) are joined together: light – darkness and lightness (levity) – weight (gravity). These merge, yielding: light (cosmic) – weight (earthly). This is the same field of tension within which the plant also grows, the level of life.

In medieval esoteric practice it was a gestalt-and-skeleton exercise, during the course of which Death (via the bones) and Life (via the marrow) were to be experienced, thus acting as a pathway into the spiritual world:

> "Behold the man of bone,
> And you behold Death.
> Look within the bones,
> And you behold the Awakener." [39]

Here, too, Rudolf Steiner establishes a connection to esoteric tradition, yet modifying and re-working the exercise to give it a contemporarily appropriate form.

As *third eurythmy meditation* we again come to a gestalt-meditation that has flowed into eurythmy from out the Esoteric School.[40] But Rudolf Steiner also spoke about it in other contexts. "The pentagram is a reality; it depicts the effects of certain currents, streaming currents of energy occurring within the etheric body of the human being. There is a particular current of energy which flows from the left foot up to a specific point of the head, from there to the right foot, from there to the left hand, then it passes through the body, through the heart to the right hand, and from there back to the left foot, so that one can inscribe the pentagram into the human being – into his head, arms, hands, legs, and feet. You must imagine this to be flows of energy, not merely a geometric figure. In the human etheric body, you really have the pentagram. The energetic effects precisely fol-

low these lines of the pentagram. These lines can undergo the most varied contortions, still they always remain a pentagram inscribed in the human body. The pentagram is an etheric reality, not a symbol but a fact."[41]

Throughout the ages, the pentagram has been experienced as the expression of the harmonic relationships (golden section) of the human gestalt within a closed figure with the heart-region as center. The point in the head – both arms – both feet; these five extremities of the gestalt form the points of the geometric figure. Even Leonardo da Vinci knew of and applied the human pentagram, with its narrower stance between the feet, the hands at the same height as the diaphragm. In the exercise the five-star is built up step by step, accompanied by sentences that are to be inwardly filled with soul-content; beginning with the feet, first the left – then the right; to the hands, into which one gazes, to the left – then to the right; then to the head, upon which both hands are placed. The exercise is concluded with the arms crossed over the heart, with the "reverence-*E (a)*", the final two lines of the verse, and the feeling: "Strength flows into my heart."

Here again the gestalt-geometry is internalized, clearly filled with soul-activity. The effect is a harmonization of body and soul, with a source of stillness in the heart:

> "*Steadfast*, I'll stand in the world
> With *certainty*, I'll tread the path of life
> *Love* I'll cherish in the depth of my being
> *Hope* shall be in all my deeds
> *Confidence* I'll impress into all my thinking
> These *five* guide me to my goal
> These *five* give me my *existence*."

> *("Standhaft *stell' ich mich ins Dasein*
> Sicher *schreite ich die Lebensbahn*
> Liebe *heg' ich im Wesenskern*
> Hoffnung *leg' ich in jegliches Tun*
> Vertrauen *präg' ich in alles Denken*
> Diese Fünf *führen mich ans Ziel*
> Diese Fünf *gaben mir das* Dasein.")* [42]

49

In one variation of the exercise, colors play a role, in that each of the five qualities is to be experienced in a different color. The pentagram corresponds to the currents flowing within the etheric body from the head into the feet, and then into the hands by way of the heart. [43]

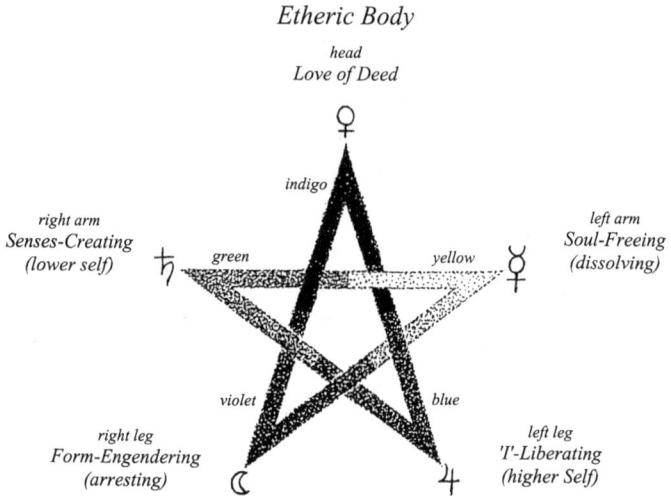

Etheric Body

head
Love of Deed

♀

indigo

right arm
Senses-Creating
(lower self) ♄   *green*   *yellow*   ☿   left arm
Soul-Freeing
(dissolving)

violet   *blue*

right leg
Form-Engendering
(arresting) ☽   ♃   left leg
'I'-Liberating
(higher Self)

The *fourth eurythmy meditation* consists of the archetypal color-gestures carried out in standing. Rudolf Steiner gave these gestures in 1915. [44] The gestures, like letters or symbols, must be inwardly filled with soul in order to appear as color. Each color-gesture already bears within itself, as expression, the relationship of the gestalt to the surrounding world. The six basic colors lay hold of all the main chakras in the ether, and consequently bring a tremendously invigorating and very differentiated effect on the whole etheric body. In the sequence of the color-gestures as given by Steiner, a gesture at rest (blue – yellow – red) is followed by a gesture in movement (green – orange – violet), in alternation.

Here, too, only that which is of immediate concern for the eurythmy meditation will be discussed. The exact indications to color are to be found in the book by Hildegard Bittorf. [45] The right arm carries out the color-gestures in standing, on the upright gestalt.

We begin with *blue* as an enveloping mantle, to the side with the arm curved and turned towards the body; the intervening space is felt as filled between the gestalt and the arm. Emanating from the heart-region (twelve-petalled lotus flower), warmth permeates and envelops the etheric source of movement in the solar plexus (ten-petalled lotus flower).

Green appears in movement within the horizontal plane with the outstretched arm, moving outwards to the side and returning. The middle region of the soul, wellspring of all color-expression, is at rest, simply observing and sensing this wide-open yet at the same time restricted gesture. The intention streams from the heart-region; it is precisely the green and its gesture that appears at the level of the shoulders, where the instrument of movement manifests within the physically perceptible world as in the first position of "I think speech".

With *yellow* we meet a gesture which is initiated from the heart, and at the same time passes through the heart, stretching outwards to the front and above. The gesture appears in extended quietude, and has to be continually renewed from within. Here, too, the heart is the source of the gesture, but this time leading upwards into the light, coming into contact with the upper chakras.

Orange blazes actively upwards and to the front, flaming out from the heart in a rushing tempo; but it also returns again to the heart, having taken in impressions from the surroundings, a gesture at rest. It is like an enthusiastic calling out, followed by an attentive listening activity that unfolds in the withdrawal. Here the heart chakra is experienced as possessing a particularly breathing quality.

Red as gesture reaches out from the heart upwards over the head, the hand open and the palm turned towards the heavens. You experience energy streaming through your whole gestalt, right down to the feet. The red appears as capital and base of the upright pillar. The crown-chakra (thousand-petalled lotus flower) is addressed from the heart and is led back to the root-chakra (four-petalled lotus flower). It is a strong, quiet gesture.

The gesture of *violet* begins from above and follows the falling arm, experiencing the weight of the arm, thus at the same time mastering heaviness. The gesture continues swinging gently, like a peaceful pendulum. Here the gesture is carried out only by using your own experienced weight, devoid of your own initiative. From the heart it is feelingly sensed how the movement is filled with weight. Again, it is the heart-chakra that is active, but everything is involved, from the solar plexus down to the root-chakra (from the twelve-petalled, to the ten-petalled, to the four-petalled lotus flower).

The series of archetypal color-gestures, carried out in standing, is the only eurythmy meditation initiated exclusively from the heart-chakra, revitalizing it again and again, and integrating, color for color, the impulses of the other chakras. By means of these strict gestures and bearing, a richly-differentiated ensoulment of the etheric body can be brought about.

The *fifth eurythmy meditation* is the first and only word-meditation in which the word is actually done in eurythmy. Historically, it is the first word which eurythmy came to know. The unfolding of the sounds evolves into a process which takes hold of the whole gestalt, preparing it to open itself to the cosmos:

Hallelujah.

Rudolf Steiner accompanies this joyful outburst with the words, "I cleanse myself of all that hinders my perceiving the Highest."[46] Here we are considering the exercise only as done in standing; as soon as it is moved in space, it changes in character, "it becomes bacchantic"!

With the *H* the soul is freed, opening itself in order to receive the divine light in astonishment via the *A (ah)*. The actual cleansing process, penetrating the entire gestalt, is accomplished by the seven-fold growing *L*, beginning around the solar plexus and finally streaming over the whole gestalt. The process is consolidated in the *E (a)* and, united with the 'I' (the ego), is impressed upon the gestalt. The next three great *L*-gestures purify the human sheaths. With the *U*, communion with the spirit is attained. The *J*, or *I*, leads over, joyfully free, into the *A (ah)* which is opened to the heavens; and the *H* draws the spirit to itself, powerfully, so that the person carrying it out may feel himself or herself to be completely permeated with it. The process passes from weight into light, filling itself with light and warmth, purging the etheric body and clarifying the soul. The growing *L*'s cause the etheric body, blossoming forth, to flood the entire gestalt.

In this exercise the journey from the center to the periphery, as process, is the crucial thing. It consolidates the etheric body.

Yet another exercise belongs here, in which the qualities of center and periphery are experienced in sudden interchange. The exercise is given as a meditation in Rudolf Steiner's lecture-course on curative education, "Within me is God" (in the evening), "I am in God" (in the morning). [47]

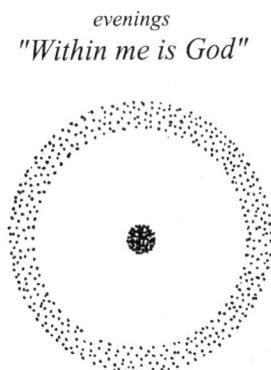

mornings	*evenings*
"I am in God"	*"Within me is God"*

In the evenings, the soul is experienced as being in the enveloping yellow periphery, with the blue center at rest within.

In the mornings, the soul is experienced as being in the yellow center, and round about the blue sheath is experienced as the source of trust and strength.

The one time, the soul is concentrated in the center, identifying with the yellow and experiencing in the surrounding blue the divine light as an all-embracing protective security. The other time, the soul identifies with the yellow periphery, experiencing the blue of the divine light within itself. Here the soul experiences itself free of the constraints of gravity and the sensory world, completely absorbed by a realm of inwardness of soul and spirit. Guided by the heart-chakra, the soul expands, breathing between center and periphery. The exercise can also be done eurythmically as counter-movement, based solely upon contraction and expansion (gestalt and gesture moving in opposing directions). This invigorates the soul, filling it with confidence and peace. The etheric body, weaving as a totality, strengthens the gestalt, filling it with light, making it whole.

The *sixth eurythmy meditation* is probably the one that is most widely practiced. Here, too, Steiner establishes a connection to esoteric tradition. He adopts the gestalt-exercise from Agrippa of Nettesheim, changing the order within the sequence, thereby making it contemporarily effective. Later on, this is augmented by corresponding texts for the six positions:

> "I think speech
> I speak
> I have spoken
> I seek for myself in the Spirit
> I feel myself within myself
> I am on the way to the spirit – to myself."

> *("Ich denke die Rede*
> *Ich rede*
> *Ich habe geredet*
> *Ich suche mich im Geiste*
> *Ich fühle mich in mir*
> *Ich bin auf dem Wege zum Geiste – zu mir.")* [48]

The exercise is treated extensively in my book *Ich denke die Rede* [49], and it also appears as the central exercise in the book *Enlivening the Chakra of the Heart* by Florin Lowndes. [50] Only one aspect, that of meditation, will be explored here.

This gestalt-exercise addresses the human being within his supersensible members. The transformation unfolds from position to position from the 'I', in order to develop the higher human being – Life-Spirit on the level of Spirit-Self – the Angel-Man, who is capable of maintaining himself, taking his place within the cosmos. This is the exercise that accompanies eurythmists in their daily work as a constant companion, aiding them in the development of their eurythmic instrument of movement. We have shown here, in its archetypal form, the level in which the human being of the future can reach the full unfolding of eurythmy.

During the course of the exercise, all the chakras are addressed. It is always the 'I', working through the heart-chakra (twelve-petalled lotus flower), that is the source of eurythmy meditation.

In the *first position* the physical instrument is experienced within space; the point of intersection lies at the level of the shoulders. The upright human being rises above the heaviness of earth. The root-chakra (four-petalled lotus flower) is addressed.

In the *second position* the etheric body takes over guiding the movement. The larynx marks the upper boundary of the "breathing human being", who speaks through movement (sixteen-petalled lotus flower).

In the *third position* the movement is guided by the soul; the diaphragm, as lower boundary, is addressed; the heart-chakra (twelve-petalled lotus flower) acts as center.

In the *fourth position* the 'I' lays hold of the will via the etheric movement center (ten-petalled lotus flower). The 'I'-directed "human being of speech" comes to birth. The soul breathes freely, both upwards and outwards into the cosmos, as well as downwards, right through the earth.

In the *fifth position* the higher human being is born. The 'I' leads the soul from the cosmos back to the gestalt. The crown-chakra (thousand-petalled lotus flower) is affected. The higher Self becomes the source of movement, guided by laws of soul and spirit.

In the *sixth position* the etheric human being is as instrument completely at the disposal of the'I'. It is possible to work eurythmically in a free manner, out of the spiritual tableau. The etheric laws have become mastered as a basis. The entire etheric body, together with all of its energy-centers, has been worked through. When in future times this will finally be attained, eurythmy will have come to its full unfolding.

We can well experience that it is precisely the meditation "I think speech" which can act as a kind of leitmotif-exercise for eurythmy practice. The eurythmic instrument is trained and prepared in stages. The movement, initially led from the center, evolves in quality to a level on which – from a higher consciousness – the periphery governs the eurythmic fashioning.

The *seventh eurythmy meditation* combines the elements of music and the spoken word. When he gave it in 1924, Steiner refers to it as an "esoteric intermezzo"[51]

TAO

TAO, perhaps the oldest mystery-word, has always contained the human being's direct relationship to the gods. Here, too, Rudolf Steiner transforms it into a eurythmy meditation suitable for the modern age, one that will accompany us far into the future. The exercise has already been discussed regarding its structure, its relationship to *IAO*, and with the forces of the Christ-Impulse in connection with wonder, compassion, and conscience. As a eurythmy meditation, however, *TAO* takes its place at the conclusion of the series.

The creative forces of the past, present and future live within this exercise. By combining notes [tones] and intervals with the vowels, music and speech are taken up in an integrated fashion. Working from the periphery, out of the cosmos, the exercise lays hold of the soul, guiding the movements. It tunes the instrument, making the forming movement supple.

By means of the gestures the soul is awakened, from the crown-chakra (thousand-petalled lotus flower) down into the heart-chakra (twelve-petalled lotus flower), responding with wonder and compassion right down to the solar plexus (ten-petalled lotus flower). Light and warmth resonate within the etheric body.

It has no doubt become apparent that all the eurythmy meditations have an esoteric source and a mystery-tradition upon which Rudolf Steiner builds by bringing each exercise into a new form that is suitable for the present age. The only exception is the archetypal color-gestures, which are directly related to the zodiacal gestures and are an immediate result of Steiner's own research.

All the meditations have their source in the region of the heart, endeavoring to become active in various ways to aid the coming to birth of the etheric human being, the "Angel-Man". Physical laws have to be superseded by the laws of the etheric world. In this lies the cultural task of eurythmy.

Chapter 9

The Meditation for Eurythmists

Towards the end of the speech-eurythmy lecture-course, [52] Rudolf Steiner gives a meditation for eurythmy, introducing it with the following words. "It is only by repeatedly calling up a certain mood of soul that the eurythmist can gain the receptivity of feeling and perception necessary for expressive gesture. This delicate and fine perception can be awakened in the eurythmist by means of a meditation drawn from the secret nature of the human organization [...] When you have meditated upon such words as these, you will discover that you can say of yourselves, 'It is as though I have awakened out of a cosmic sleep into the heavenly realm of eurythmy.'"

"I seek within me

the activity of creative forces,

the life of creative powers.

The earthly force of weight

speaks to me

through the word of my feet;

The forming might of the air

speaks to me

through the singing of my hands;

The power of heavenly light

speaks to me

through the thinking of my head,

how the world in the human being

speaks, sings, thinks."

[tr. Alan Stott]

("Ich suche im Innern
Der schaffenden Kräfte Wirken,
Der schaffenden Mächte Leben.
Es sagt mir
Der Erde Schweremacht
Durch meiner Füsse Wort,
Es sagt mir
Der Lüfte Formgewalt
Durch meiner Hände Singen,
Es sagt mir
Des Himmels Lichteskraft
Durch meines Hauptes Sinnen,
Wie die Welt im Menschen
Spricht, singt, sinnt.")

We encounter a clearly differentiated structure in the mantram, consisting of three introductory opening lines, then the threefold sounding of "[It] speaks to me" embracing the whole threefold human being, and the two concluding lines as a summary. This threefold pulse guides us along the following path. Taking my own self as the point of departure, "I seek within me", I then proceed to the threefold "[It] speaks to me" as cosmic answer; and in closing, I experience their union, "how the world in the human being / speaks, sings, thinks". My own activity is directed to search towards "the secret nature of the human organization"; there then appears out the periphery, objectively (*"Es sagt mir"* –"[It] speaks to me"), the threefold differentiated manner in which I meet the world through my body, and how this cosmically-creative world is revealed to me – in speaking, singing, and thinking. Within the "It" *("Es")* there weaves Cosmic Will, Cosmic Feeling and Cosmic Thinking, actively working through my gestalt.

Within the realm of space and time, facing earthly heaviness, "the earthly force of weight", and *"in overcoming"*[53] this weight by making use of my earth-bound limbs for movement, I lay claim to my capacity for eurythmy speaking.

Through the air's formative power, "the forming might of the air", I experience within my soul my eurythmy singing, by using my arms as the free organs of expression to form gestures *"in relation to"* [54] the air.

Through cosmic light, "the power of heavenly light", in a state of heightened awareness, I am able to apply my senses and my thinking *"with respect to"* Intuition's light of consciousness, in order to lay hold of those form-giving forces within my own eurythmic fashioning.

This pertains to eurythmy as a whole, not yet differentiated into speech-eurythmy and music-eurythmy. "The word of my feet", in walking and moving through space, reveals the movement in time inherent in the temporal structures of language and music. "The singing of my hands" reveals in flowing gesture-forms a eurythmy speaking and singing which is filled with soul. "The thinking of my head" reveals the creating out of the tableau-consciousness of a wholeness in speech and music in eurythmy.

"In overcoming ..." is the key to all formative activity working with the resistance of weight of our instrument of movement.
"In relation to ..." is the key to all artistic work seeking to bring expressive gestures into artistic relation.
"With respect to ..." is the key to all attempts at forming an artistically balanced wholeness.

The Language of the Will

A notebook entry of Steiner's runs:
> The language of ideation – spoken language,
> The language of feeling – music,
> The language of the will – eurythmy.

The language of the will has to do with the "human being of movement" as expression of the will. In eurythmy we are dealing with conscious, ensouled movement. It's true home is at the threshold where the daytime-'I' crosses over into the heightened awareness of a tableau-consciousness, to an Imaginative consciousness, out of which it is possible to act, to form and to move. It might be helpful at this point to consider two occasions on which Steiner speaks about human movement as the manifestation of will which the human being, 'I'-filled, initiates from outside, out of the periphery.

"In willing, I reach outside my body, and I move by means of forces external to me [...] You don't raise your leg by using forces located within yourself, but you lift your leg by applying forces that really are active from outside; the same holds true for the arm [...] We immerse ourselves in the world, we surrender ourselves to the world in our will." [55]

After a lecture in Berlin, held in October, 1908, when eurythmy, as a gift of destiny, was knocking on the portal of earthly existence but was not yet granted admittance, Rudolf Steiner spoke with Margarita Woloschin concerning the rhythms of the heavenly bodies and the rhythms of the bodily limbs. He said to her, "In your dancing there is an independent rhythm. Dance is a movement in which the center lies outside the human being. The rhythm of the dance reaches back to the most distant cosmic ages, to the state of Duration prior to Saturn [...]"[56]

In the meditation, Steiner differentiates this force working in from the periphery. It works through earthly weight from below, out of the periphery through the forming might of the air, from above through the power of light, through the human gestalt. There arises before us the image of a meditation we have already discussed, "Light streams upwards / Weight presses downwards." [57]

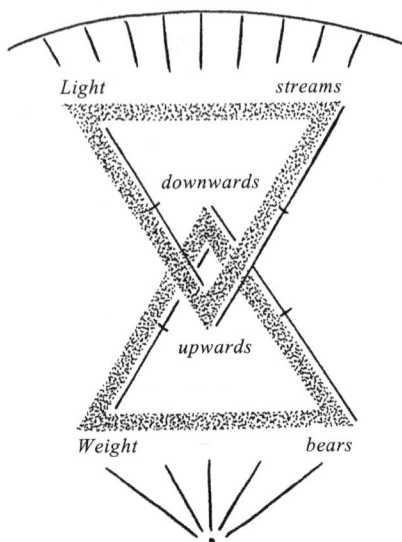

Light

> Light streams upwards into the periphery,
> towards the light of the heavens.

Warmth

> Warmth builds up between the polar extremes,
> as the free space for movement within the gestalt.

Weight

> Weight bears downwards, to the center of the earth;
> in opposition, the human power to achieve the
> upright position arises.

That is the microcosmic aspect, through which the influence of cosmic forces manifests on the human gestalt. Macrocosmically, the heights and the depths harmonize in the etheric world with the periphery.

The Heights
> Together with the heights, the heavens, there sound the forces of the heights, of light.

The Periphery
> Together with the periphery, the widths, the forces of the periphery, of warmth are at work

The Depths
> Together with the depths, the earth's center, there sound the forces of the earth, of weight.

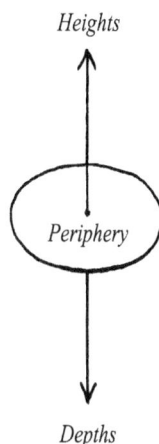

Heights

Periphery

Depths

It is within these etheric dimensions that eurythmy takes its source; it is but brought to appearance via the bodily instrument within three-dimensional space.

The primordial basis of all human gesture, contraction and expansion – laughing and crying in the realm of expressive movement – is manifested in three archetypal phenomena, which harmonize with the threefold nature of this meditation.

"Life-breathing" [or "the breathing of life"] as the pure expression of the will ranging from initiating impulse to finished form, is active in "the word of my feet". "Life-breathing" joins the body to life – that which has already become with that which is still becoming – in expressive gesture.

"Warmth-breathing" [or "the breathing of warmth"] as the expression of feeling, breathing between the warmth of connecting bonds and the cold of isolation, is related to "the singing of my hands" in expressive gestures. "Warmth-breathing" joins together life and soul; ensouled movement unfolds as sphere [atmosphere] around the gestalt.

63

"Light-breathing" [or "the breathing of light"], the appearance of the gesture within a particular zone, breathes between light and darkness, joy and sorrow, and truth and goodness, revealing "the thinking of my head". "Light-breathing" joins the soul to the spirit, to the intention of the movement.

"Light-breathing" – the breathing of light between heaven and earth – is where eurythmic movement originates as *intention*. It then appears as zone on the human gestalt in the struggle of "life-breathing" with the earthly forces of weight. And in "warmth-breathing" there lives the connection to the cosmic periphery [as *sphere*]. [58]

The human being between the light and the earth raises himself into the upright, and begins to walk. He can ensoul the movement with feeling, and make his instrument of movement permeable [transparent]. The supporting resistance of the earth, and the earthly force of weight, are both necessary for the development of these human abilities.

Through the "life-breathing", the 'I' lays hold of the will – the consolidating or liberating movement – and via the etheric body, it takes the physical body along with this direction of will. These are the forces of life, which allow the living movement to manifest as movement guided out of the light, out of the intention. It is the "warmth-breathing" that enables the movement to become soul-filled gesture, seeking the connection to the world in moods of color, and in being inwardly affected by something.

The *three artistic means* – as described by Rudolf Steiner for the speech-sounds – are also addressed in this triadic meditation:
> To "the word of my feet" there corresponds the *"movement, which conveys soul-content"*.
> To "the singing of my hands" there comes the *"feeling* experienced in meeting the outer world".
> To "the thinking of my head", the *"character*, revealed from within outwards", builds the whole gesture as it manifests. [59]

One last indication regarding the threefold nature of this meditation should be mentioned. It concerns the *three primary sources of movement* within the human being:

64

All *movement* has its source in the solar plexus, in the central focus of the autonomic nervous system, within our 'I' in willing.

All *soul-filled movement* has its source within the region of the heart, in the center for our feeling of the 'I'.

All *intentional design* originates in the region around the focal point on the forehead, the seat of the 'I'-concept. [60]

The correlation with the chakras has already been discussed in the treatment of the eurythmy meditations. The ten-petalled lotus flower, allied with the four-petalled lotus flower (root-chakra), is connected with the solar plexus. The twelve-petalled lotus flower is connected with the heart-region, and the two-petalled lotus flower with the forehead.

Mighty forces, weaving throughout the etheric cosmos – the heights, depths, and periphery – speak to the human being via his instrument of movement, and there arises a dynamic image of the Word. Man as the being of the Word, made in the image of the divine Logos-forces, can allow the movement thereby ensouled to speak and to sing. He or she sets free the Logos-forces out of himself or herself, letting them manifest according to etheric laws *through* and *in* the visible movement.

"The activity of creative forces" and *"the life of creative powers"* are the revelations which "I seek within me"! These are the words with which the meditation for eurythmists begins.

Who are these forces and powers? They are those Beings who, through the zodiac and the planets, form man as a being of the Word. It is the working and weaving of the Logos-forces in the etheric world. The Sun-secret is revealed by the dynamic etheric laws in the ensouled, eurythmic movement.

Rudolf Steiner characterizes this process of development as follows:
"The attempt has been made to provide mankind with something, which, so to speak, already outwardly shows evolution, the sense and spirit of evolution. That could only be accomplished [when] one was clear that even in the everyday world, in concrete daily life, we

also live in a world of forms, and that striding ahead, walking forwards, means penetrating into the world of movement. The world of forms governs the physical body; the world of movement governs the etheric body. Those movements have to be discovered that are inherent in the etheric body. The human being has to be taught how to use gesture and movement of the physical body to express what is natural for the etheric body [...] This is attempted in eurythmy. It will become apparent that the human being really is the connecting link between the cosmic letters, the cosmic sounds, and that which we use as human speech-sounds and letters in our poetry. With eurythmy, a new art will come into being. It is an art for everyone. And one could only wish that mankind would be moved to develop an understanding for this art [...] In short, one can define eurythmy as the fulfillment of that which the human etheric body needs according to its own natural laws [...] Consequently, in eurythmy we really do have something that is an integral part of our spiritual life, and that has been conceived from out of its totality." [61]

Mighty, force-wielding beings are addressed at the beginning of the meditation. These spirits of creative forces are the Beings of the First Hierarchy influencing the human being out of the cosmos. Together with the Archai from the Third Hierarchy, they make possible the upright human nature. Correspondingly, the creative powers are Beings of the Second Hierarchy. The Dynamis, the Spirits of Movement, assist the human being in walking, in movement. The Powers, the Exusiai, brothers to the arts, are active in the air and in the breathing, in speech, and in gesture. The Kyriotetes, the Spirits of Light, work on the entirety through the human being. The gods assist man to attain his upright posture, they help him to move, but he himself must build up the new human being, the etheric human being.

I am the instrument of the Logos-forces weaving in the etheric realm. This is the Sun-secret: Not I, but Christ in me.

Chapter 10

The Three Key Archetypal Gestures of Eurythmy

Within the realm of moving forms and gestures, certain primal forms and gestures are to be found, which on the one hand are seminal for a wealth of eurythmic elements, and on the other hand are comprehensive sources of power through which all movement is qualitatively determined.

"Through the word of my feet..."
> For the world of forms it is *the straight line and the spiral*. The whole diversity of forms arises out of this pair of polar opposites.

"Through the singing of my hands..."
> For the world of *gestures* it is *contraction and expansion*, bending and stretching, laughing and crying – all gestures originate from this one archetypal gesture.

"Through the thinking of my head..."
> The third primal power can only be laid hold of indirectly. It is the power of the 'I', or ego, that unites polarities, allowing them to manifest on the physical plane as though the movements were already etheric and spiritual. It is that power through which we are able to cross the threshold to allow the movement to appear eurythmical. In crossing the bridge from "here" to "there", we discover the eurythmic fashioning. It is *the transformation of the center into the circumference* – from the periphery to the point.

Some observations by way of example will now be made in order to present a key-exercise in concrete terms, purely with the intention of arriving at inner points of reference, aids for eurythmic practice, and criteria for one's own personal appraisal. We follow the method practiced by Goethe, who claimed, "I don't cease looking till I have found a significant point from which much can be derived."

We shall begin with the third primal power: center – periphery

Eurythmically and geometrically, the *circle* is a picture for the 'I'. In day-consciousness, we feel we are wide awake within our bodies; during the night-consciousness in sleep we expand in soul and spirit to the periphery. The "I" is a twofold being, intentionally awake in its midpoint existence, and as our higher Self in a peripheral consciousness is without intention yet full of spiritual content. On the basis of this archetype, a number of eurythmic elements can be practiced, all possessing as content the dynamics of midpoint–periphery as a "breathing of the "I". In this way we can practice on the one hand the gentle transition to a delicate awakening in the periphery, and on the other hand the illumination of the "human being of movement". This formative "breathing of the 'I'" lives not only in the spatial forms but also in the gestures; it is all-pervasive, or, in other words, it unites within itself all other aspects.

In *walking* [moving] forwards and backwards, the intention has to be made visible through the gestalt in both dimensions, moving forwards and descending, moving backwards and ascending. In this way, the three sources of movement [in the solar plexus, the heart region, and the forehead] are actively trained within the stream of movement passing through the gestalt. At the same time, the sphere of touch can be experienced to the front, and the sphere of listening to the back. The movement breathes between the light-filled periphery and the earthly weight.

The next exercise is to move a *lemniscate* both in space and through the gestalt, in such a way that the front part appears to be centrally oriented, whereas the part behind appears as though united with the periphery. Using the source of eurythmic movement, we negotiate the sudden transition experienced in passing through the crossing-point. In front and inwards, the movement is guided in such a way that our own center remains radially connected to the midpoint within the lemniscate; outwards and behind, through the tangential forming coming from the periphery, our own center becomes an organ of perception. Through the sudden change occurring at the crossing-point, we experience inwardly the qualitative eurythmic "movement", and outwardly the qualitative eurythmic "feeling". The other sources of movement play a secondary role in the movement-process.

The next movement-exercise in this series, *blue* as eurythmic color-gesture, is experienced in its archetypal form as a sheltering and protecting of the body. Within, near our movement-center, the quality of color becomes brighter, more light-filled. Responding to changes in our inner activity, the same gesture can expand, becoming cosmically receptive. It is experienced as a refreshingly deep in-breathing from the periphery, open as wide as the blue of the heavens. Through inner activity, the color-gesture "blue" is changed from "movement-color" into "feeling-color" (veil color), touching the soul out of the periphery like a cloak of trust. This only succeeds in such a smooth and continuous manner with the blue conceived as the image of the cosmic ether. "The ether itself cannot be perceived, this is true, but it attains perceptibility through the great majesty with which it is placed in cosmic space, by which it is made known, is revealed, in the blue of the heavens." [62]

Contraction and expansion as such is the eurythmical and human archetypal gesture, moving in a breathing alternation between center and periphery. From his center, the middle of his soul, "the human being rises above the world" by stretching through his gestures and raying out towards the world. "Feeling his own weakness in facing the world", his gesture gives way under the overwhelming force of the impressions, he draws the impressions into himself, gathering new strength in concentration within so as to open himself to the world once more. Here gestalt and gesture move in a breathing rhythm of expression between 'I' and world. [63]

The exercise *"Behold yourself – Behold the world" ("Schau in dich – Schau um dich")* by Rudolf Steiner is the next one to be considered here. This spiral with the double curve, running horizontally to the left and winding in upon itself, then out again and to the right, forms the basis of the exercise. Following the text, the vowels are done eurythmically on the way in, and the consonants on the way out. The exercise can be built up a step at a time, allowing ever more eurythmy quality to become visible.

— First, only the form is moved, as movement in space,
— then following the form inwards and then outwards,
— then moving inward musically, flowing within the stream of time (with the current), and moving outward plastically, with strongly-contoured movements in space (against the current),
— then, in addition, the vowels on the way in, and the consonants on the way out,
— further, the goal inside the spiral has to be anticipated, and the intended goal outside equally so,
— contraction and expansion are integrated into the whole.

Center and periphery present themselves in ever greater differentiation through the movement oscillating in between. The whole exercise is imbued with the character of 'I'-feeling, which allows all the movement to appear as a breathing.

"We seek the soul – we are illumined by the spirit" ("Wir suchen die Seele – Uns strahlet der Geist") will be considered as the last example in this series of exercises given by Steiner. This exercise, too, is a spiral-exercise involving center and periphery. Moving forwards, spiraling to the center, we do the vowels in the text. Then, moving backwards after an sudden transition, we again spiral inwards, but this time as though within an enveloping sheaf of tangents out the periphery. On the way back we do the consonants in the text. Concerning the specifically eurythmic geome-

try joining together centrally-created and peripherally-created forms, both spatially and temporally, Steiner noted the following, as already mentioned above, *"Vita eurythmo-Geometrie!"* [64]

On the way to the front and inwards, the vowels seek to radiate outwards; on the way backwards and inwards, the consonants are placed outside, strongly contoured and formed from without. Like the previous exercise, this one too can be built up step by step, with increasing consolidation. This exercise possesses an 'I'-will character, demanding a wakeful, strong forming activity. With warmth we move forwards; light-filled we give form to the way back; in wakefulness we lay hold of the transformation. The vowels are of a purely dionysian nature; the consonants are apollonian in character.

For Gestures, the Key-Exercise and Primal Source is Contraction and Expansion

It can be understood as movement at the level of the etheric:

"All bending gathers auric strength from without, letting it flow inwards. A darkening of the surrounding auric space results. In bending, life-forces are used up within us; the auric energy streaming in from outside consumes the human being [...] With every stretching movement, something of the will leaves us, causing a brightening in the surrounding aura. I do something which continues, spreading outwards. [...] Stretching carries the will outwards, releasing life-forces."[65]

Actually, every human being is continually active in this manner during the course of daily events. But it is only within the context of freely-fashioned [artistic] movement that this activity is brought to visible expression.

On the soul-level, the archetypal gesture reveals a definite relation between the 'I' and the world:

"Did you know that only a being gifted with an 'I' can laugh and cry? That only the human being can, but that an animal could never laugh and cry? And so, we want to express these two possibilities, how the 'I' faces the world in laughing and crying, in two ways of forming movements, that is, through expansion and contraction." [66]

"Expansion = raising the inner over the outer"; contraction = feeling inner helplessness when facing outer facts; but a gathering of inner strength (defense).[67]

The archetypal gesture of contraction and expansion is comprised of three archetypal phenomena:

"Light-breathing", a breathing of light, as movement between the light-filled periphery above and the earth's dark center, is the artistic means of expression for all the *zones* of eurythmic activity.

"Warmth-breathing", a breathing of warmth, is opened up, with a feeling for the periphery, the wide expanses, and draws itself together, contracting into itself; it thus expresses the breathing of the soul in a *spherically* more expansive or more isolated manner.

"Life-breathing", a breathing of life, ranging from the initial impulse to the final completion of each gesture, is the artistic means of expression for manifesting *intention*.

This is outlined here only to the extent required in this context, as the primal source for all eurythmy gestures. [68]

Here too, the whole human being is addressed, with his three sources of movement:

Spiritual source of movement – In the region of the forehead-chakra
(concept of 'I').
Soul-related source of movement – In the region of the heart-chakra
(feeling of 'I').
Etheric source of movement – In the region of the solar plexus chakra
('I'-will). [69]

For the World of Forms the Key-Exercise is
the Straight Line and the Spiral

These two polar-opposite types of form are the basis for all form-creations. These are forces which are to be found in the zodiac and which come to expression in its gestures.

For eurythmy, the spiral as archetypal form begins qualitatively out in the cosmos, and ends in the region of the human heart. Since time immemorial, it has been the gesture symbolizing human evolution.

For eurythmy, the raying straight line, qualitatively speaking, also comes from the stars to the earth; but it passes, as it were, right through the human being. It comes out of the infinite, touches some point within the sense-perceptible world, and returns to the infinite.

These two archetypal forms encompass everything that can be expressed in eurythmy movement in space, at each level differentiated according to the various inner aspects.

In a lecture from 28th June, 1914, Steiner relates how forms originating in the spiritual world are able to "speak". The concept of the 'I', for example, can be experienced within a form when we progress from a knowledge of form to a feeling for form. With a circle, we will always feel the 'I', selfhood. "Feeling a circle would mean experiencing selfhood. Experiencing a circle in the horizontal plane, experiencing a sphere in space, means feeling selfhood, experiencing the 'I'."

By molding the circle into uniformly-surging waves, we express the 'I' entering into relationship with the world. This contouring of the circumference of the circle expresses a struggle, so to speak, a mutual exchange with the outer world. We feel that *the inside is stronger than the outside!*"

If the circle is divided up into evenly-distributed serrations, notches, or indentations, this too reveals a particular relation between the self and the world. "And with this jaggedly-formed circle, the outer world has bored its way in, and is stronger than that which lies within the circle." [70] *"The outer has triumphed"* summarizes our experience of the serrated circle.

In the circle of streaming, surging movement, there arise *rounded forms* when rhythmic impulses work their way into the outside world. When the rhythmic impulses drive inwards from the periphery, then *straight forms* result, working their way into the circle.

This can also be observed in nature, in the realm of life, as an expression of the etheric world, for example, in the forms of plant leaves. In eurythmy, these archetypal forms arising from the circle are the rudimentary basis out of which everything else is developed.

The *geometric form-structures* constitute the next stage in the development of eurythmic forms:
The straight-line, ray-like forms are: triangle, rectangle, pentagon, hexagon, and heptagon (seven-pointed star).
The curving, spiraling forms are: circle, spiral, lemniscate, and harmonious eight.

These forms act as structures in, for example, the silent preludes *(Auftakte)*, establishing their character; or they appear like a crystal in the midst of otherwise flowing forms, speaking eloquently as geometric figures; they also appear in educational eurythmy-exercises.

The spiral is also an exercise in its own right, as already described in the exercises "Behold thyself – behold the world" and "We seek the soul – we are illumined by the spirit". The exercise of Continuous Eights (never-ending lemniscate) is a circle-dance; the triangle is the basic form-element in both the Energy Dance and the Peace Dance. Indeed, in many educational eurythmy-exercises it is precisely the geometric forms that provide the foundation.

Eurythmy is also familiar with yet another, quite different form-building aspect, that of what we call *dionysian and apollonian forms*:
In the *dionysian forms*, everything is experienced out of the midpoint, my midpoint facing the world, which is often also centrally oriented in space [that is, directed towards the center of the form]. Whether considering the forms for "I–You–He" or those for "Think-

ing–Feeling–Will", it is always radiating and spiraling forces that build both types of forms. The essential difference lies in changing the standpoint taken while moving the forms from myself to the world.

So, too, in the circle-exercise for "He"-forms, "He who illumines the clouds" *("Der Wolkendurchleuchter"),* I seek the connection between myself and the periphery, supported by the circle's shared center. All circle-dances ultimately return to their starting-point, incorporate the circle with its center as the ordering principle.

The *apollonian forms* come about through the movement relationship being frontally orientated between "behind", receiving light, and "in front", world-forming.

In eurythmy, the apollonian forms are also referred to as the *"grammatical forms"* for nouns (concrete, abstract, *"wesenhaft"* – "beingness", condition) and verbs (active, passive, and all the nuances in between).

Here, too, we have to do with raying and spiraling forces, out of which the forms are fashioned. Here, too, the decisive factor is the interplay of different standpoints, alternating between a world of spiritual beings (behind) and a visible, tangible world (in front).

The source of the forms is always the same. The form-structures are all derived from the etheric principle of "inner" and "outer", each acquiring its specific quality as a result of the respective inner attitude regarding the world.

This etheric substance appears with a special clarity in *Rudolf Steiner's forms for poetry and music.* They can be conceived as thought-movements, as the comprehensive etheric framework or time-structure inherent in the poetic or musical substance of a particular work of art. It is truly a path of schooling, gradually to feel our way into these etheric figures in space (poetry), and these etheric tracings in time (music). One possible approach is gradually to expand our feeling-consciousness from speech-sound transitions to word-gestures, from single images and motifs to lines and periods; we thereby lay hold of the first comprehensive units. We then progress from verses, stanzas and musical phrasing to the total structure of a piece, out of which the work of art can manifest in the movement-form.

An enormous effort is needed in order to be able to immerse oneself in the tableau of the whole. Each poem and each piece of music possesses its own movement-form, its own structure in time, which can be taken hold of in the eurythmic form as thought-movement. This structural totality then becomes visible as movement in space, "on" and "through" the moving gestalt of the eurythmist. It becomes discernable in its effects on and around the ensouled movement-gestalt.

The "how" of a movement's execution becomes a question of artistic design, whether it is a movement between center and periphery, remaining held or ranging through the widths of the periphery, proceeding from oneself or being formed by the world. In eurythmy fashioning, all three forces live and work together – the raying and spiraling movement-forms, the gestures breathing between contraction and expansion, and the "breathing of the 'I'", alternating between a condition of dreamy sleep and a state of intense wakefulness. [71]

Chapter 11

All the Vowels taken together are the Complete Human Being

In the lecture of 9th January, 1915, Rudolf Steiner discusses the human being who speaks and sings. The etheric body is predisposed to accompany such activities with eurythmic movements, but it is hindered by the body; it is restrained by Ahriman. Through eurythmic movements, the attempt is made to draw out that movement which the 'I' can produce within the etheric body:

"We are trying to wrest this eurythmy out of Ahriman's grasp; for it is because Ahriman entered into the world that the human etheric body became so hardened that it could not develop eurythmy as a natural gift. Human beings would all be doing eurythmy, if Ahriman had not hardened the human etheric body so much that the eurythmic element cannot come to expression [...]"

For clairvoyant consciousness, the complete human being is manifested in certain movement-forms when all the vowels are heard.

"*A, E, I, O, U* – is always a complete human being, in fact a spectrum, an etheric specter of the complete human being. But only such that the etheric body is moved in a one-sided way, so that when you listen to someone speaking '*A, E, I, O, U*' this occurs in such a manner that you see five persons spectrally, one after the other, always with a different movement-form and such that the complete human being is not always fully and equally visible but rather sometimes more the head, or more the hands, or more the legs. The other bodily parts then retreat, as it were, into darkness and obscurity." [72]

The eurythmic gesture for *A (ah)* expresses the soul-mood of astonishment, of wonder. *A* is "the human being full of wonder, who

77

amazes himself, astonished by his own true being; man marveling at himself – actually the human being in his highest, most ideal unfolding." [73]

The eurythmic gesture for *E (a)* expresses the soul-mood of self-reliance in facing another person, of being affected and holding one"'s ground. "In E we are affected and nevertheless maintain ourselves [our upright] – a self-preservation in the face of being affected."[74]

The eurythmic gesture for *I (ee)* expresses the soul-mood of self-affirmation, of consolidating the spirit within ourselves. The human being "wants to express self-affirmation; he wishes to claim his place in the world."[75]

The eurythmic gesture for *O* expresses the soul-mood of love, of devotion to another being. "The *O*-mood is that of embracing, of taking something up into yourself, of incorporating it. You therefore need light colors."[76]

The eurythmic gesture for *U (oo)* expresses the soul-mood of fear and longing. "The *U* [...] can be experienced as that which inwardly chills, stiffens, paralyses in the soul [...] where you freeze. In short, *U* is that which chills, and stiffens ."[77] In *U* the "human soul enters into a relationship with events occurring above the earthly realm, beyond its own experience, that actually does not concern it at all." [78]

Rudolf Steiner's eurythmy-figures for the vowels illustrate in color and form the way in which the sound-gestures appear eurythmically on the gestalt. [79]

The *A (ah)*, in reddish-lilac, with a greenish-blue veil and light red character, opens up from the middle region of the human being, which is strongly emphasized by the veil with its downward-directed gesture. The *E (a)*, in green with a light yellow veil and pale red character, appears energetically crossed at shoulder-level. The *I (ee)*, in yellow-orange with a red veil and gentle blue character, reveals a wakeful, controlled gesture pointing upwards beyond the gestalt, and at the same time restrained below; the head itself expresses once more the bearing or gesture of self-affirmation. The *O*, reddish with a greenish-yellow veil and blue character appears as a rounded gesture remarkably far down in front of the gestalt, as if held in devotion. The *U*, in blue with a yellow stole-like veil streaming over the gestalt from above and with purple character, appears narrowly compressed and directed downwards in front of the gestalt.

In the lecture of 21st February, 1924, Rudolf Steiner links the musical scale with spoken language by means of the vowels. [80] He introduces a correspondence which he adopts from Josef Matthias Hauer, who apparently developed it purely from listening. In addition, Steiner brings the degrees of the scale [keynote-related intervals] into relation with the vowels. The human gestalt resonates like an ensouled monochord, with the prime sounding in the legs in *U*. The second appears in correspondence with the abdomen in the *O*-gesture. The third degree of the scale harmonizes with the region of the chest in the *A (ah)*-gesture. Within the series of the main vowels, the level of the mouth [and throat] localizes the fifth degree of the scale with the *E (a)*- gesture as the corresponding speech-sound. The seventh degree of the scale brings us to the region of the forehead and the corresponding speech-sound *I (ee)*. The octave, via the skull, brings the gestalt to completion, at the same time completing the scale; it resonates in the corresponding speech-sound *U*, the prime on a higher level.

Now let us attempt to summarize the aspects described, letting them harmonize together: the soul-mood of the vowel, the image of the speech-sound in the eurythmy-figure, and the correlation between the gestalt and the corresponding speech-sound.

When living into the eurythmic *A (ah)*, we experience our "human middle" particularly vividly, as it opens from the region of the heart towards the regions below. In A the soul lives in wonder, out of the heart-chakra.

When living in the eurythmic *E (a)*-gesture, maintaining ourselves – our upright – as we face the world, the region of the larynx is affected. The larynx-chakra then appears full of light.

In the eurythmic *I (ee)*-gesture, we take hold of the entire gestalt in self-affirmation. The head chakra in particular lights up in wakefulness.

The *O* in the eurythmic-gesture lives within our feelings as compassion. The area around the solar plexus (the ten-petalled lotus flower) sounds brightly, like the musical second.

The *U* in the eurythmic-gesture, with its enclosed nature and in its streaming directed towards the earth, unites the human being with a spirituality beyond its own nature. Like the prime, it corresponds to the root-chakra, and illuminates the "lower man".

The human aura becomes brighter as a result of performing the vowels, in sequence, moving upwards from the heart into the head and then downwards into the feet. This phenomenon, verifiable by everyone, is also a eurythmic meditation. It is a way in which ancient gnostic wisdom can be laid hold of afresh. [81] For eurythmy, it provides a solid basis for a spiritual anthropology.

Chapter 12

Further Suggestions for Meditative Work in Eurythmy

The eurythmic meditations are the formative power, as it were, for making our instrument receptive and permeable, remolding it for eurythmy. The series presented here is intended to furnish a basis for eurythmic work. No doubt everyone who has been working eurythmically for years has his or her own individual exercises, in addition to the classic meditations described here. For example, living for a period of time concentrating entirely upon one particular speech-sound until it reveals something of it secrets. Or, by means of a brief series of gestures, to unite yourself with your instrument and with the eurythmic space.

Rudolf Steiner's poetical work *The Twelve Moods* [82] can also be approached meditatively in a variety of ways. In this regard, in a lecture on the occasion of the first performance of the zodiac and planets, he offers the following encouragement:

"There is to be found in each verse precisely that mood which corresponds to the respective planet as it appears in the heavens [...] Although the general mood of the verse is maintained in every single line, you will, in each of the lines corresponding to Mars within the seven-line series [of the individual verses], nevertheless recognize the Mars-mood within the line. So that actually the ideal would be that if someone were to be awakened from sleep and a line were to be read to him: 'In becoming, action persists' *('Im Werden verharret Wirken')* – that he would say: 'Of course, Mars in Scorpion!' And at another line:'Jupiter in the Scales', and so on. So you see, this is the very opposite of any kind of subjective arbitrariness. It is really taking seriously our oneness with the laws of the universe." [83]

And so, everyone can develop his or her individual manner of working with the verses and the planetary verse-lines. You can, for example, work to awaken a verse to inner life during the corresponding four-week period of the year, possibly by cultivating each verse-line on its respective day of the week. This can be attained by eurythmically experiencing the corresponding consonant of the verse in a distinctive manner for each line. The speech-sound, carried out in this way from one line to the next, allows the sound to be formed in quite vital and varied ways. The color of the zodiacal sign serves as a fundamental background; the color of each planetary line in the verse colors the dynamic mood differently each time.

Some further suggestions for inwardly bringing to life the mystery of language could be: Doing the vowels in the planetary coloring of the respective line; doing the consonants in each line in the coloring of the verse's zodiacal gesture; experiencing the verbs and their varying importance; experiencing the different forms of speech within the zodiacal round (imperative – indicative – subjunctive).

"One really tries to live into this here, into the mood, in the doing, living into everything, and – one would like to say – that what you have seen happening here gives you the possibility of developing the necessary agility and ideas which are mobile regarding what one may call:

> The Word surges through the World,
> And the World Formation holds the Word fixed."

> *("Das Wort wallt durch die Welt,*
> *Und die Weltenbildung hält das Wort fest.")* [84]

Endnotes

N/T = not translated;   E.T. = English translation in typescript

1. See R. Bock, 'The Point and the Circle', in *Newsletter from the Section for the Arts of Eurythmy, Speech and Music*, No. 27, Dornach, January 1997, pp. 20-22.

2. Rudolf Steiner, *From the History & Contents of the First Section of the Esoteric School 1904-1914*. GA 264. Anthroposophic Press, 1998, p. 166.

3. Ibid., *emphases added by W. B.*

4. Rudolf Steiner, *Eurythmy as Visible Speech*. GA 279. Rudolf Steiner Press, London 1984. Lecture, Dornach, 11th July, 1924. *Emphases added by W. B.*

5. GA 264 (see endnote 2), p. 167.

6. GA 264 (see endnote 2), p. 168.

7. GA 279 (see endnote 4), lecture of 24th June, 1924. E.T. in typescript, Rudolf Steiner Library, Ghent, NY.

8. Rudolf Steiner, *Bilder okkulter Siegel und Säulen*. GA 284, lecture of 21st May, 1907. N/T.

9. Rudolf Steiner, *Zur Geschichte und aus den Inhalten der erkenntniskultischen Abteilung der Esoterischen Schule von 1904 bis 1914*. GA 265, Dornach 1987. N/T.

10. GA 284 (see endnote 8), p. 65.

11. GA 265 (see endnote 9), p. 456.

12. Ibid., p. 460.

13. Ibid., p. 478.

14. GA 284 (see endnote 8), lecture of 24th October, 1914. E.T. in typescript R 61, Rudolf Steiner Library, London.

15. Rudolf Steiner, lecture of 30th December, 1921, in *Stilformen des Organisch-Lebendigen*. Dornach 1933 (not yet published in the Complete Works). N/T. Appears as a single lecture in *Rosicrucianism and Modern Initiation,* lecture 5, Rudolf Steiner Press, London.

16. Hilde Raske, *The Language of Colour*, Rudolf Steiner's painting and the artistic windows in the First Goetheanum. Walter Keller Verlag, Dornach, n. d.

17. The sketch of the curtain for eurythmy done by Rudolf Steiner has been reproduced in: Hilde Raske, *The Language of Colour* (see endnote 16); see also Lea van der Pals, "Thoughts on Rudolf Steiner's 'Eurythmy Curtain' Pastel", in Newsletter from the Section for the Arts of Eurythmy, Speech and Music, No. 29. Dornach, Michaelmas 1998, p. 35f.

18. Rudolf Steiner, *Die Entstehung und Entwicklung der Eurythmie*. GA 277a. 2nd ed. Dornach 1982, p. 18 (E.T. in preparation).

19. Rudolf Steiner, lecture of 30th December, 1921, in Ibid.

20. Ibid.

21. Lecture of 17th July, 1923, in Rudolf Steiner, *Eurythmie*. Dornach 1991 (not yet published in the Collected Works). N/T.

22. Ibid.

23. Ibid.

24. Rudolf Steiner, *Earthly and Cosmic Man*, GA 133, lecture of 14th May, 1922. Garber Communications Inc., 1986.

25. Rudolf Steiner, *Eurythmy as Visible Singing*, GA 278, lecture of 23rd February, 1924. Anderida Music Trust, Stourbridge 1999.

26. Rudolf Steiner, *Curative Eurythmy*, GA 315, lecture of 12th April, 1921. Rudolf Steiner Press, London 1983.

27. See Rudolf Steiner, *Entstehung und Entwicklung der Eurythmie*. GA 277a, Dornach 1982, and Annemarie Dubach, *The Basic Principles of Eurythmy*. Mercury Press, Spring Valley, 1996.

28. Ibid.

29. Rudolf Steiner, *The Easter Festival in the Evolution of the Mysteries*, GA 233a, lecture of 22nd April, 1924. Rudolf Steiner Press / Anthroposophic Press 1988.

30. Rev. 1: 8, English rendering from the tr. of Emil Bock, *Das Neue Testament*. Urachhaus, Stuttgart.

31. Rudolf Steiner, *Guidance in Esoteric Training*, GA 245, Rudolf Steiner Press, London 1998, p. 32.

32. The Foundation Stone Meditation and its rhythms as presented during the Christmas Conference 1923/24, in: Rudolf Steiner, *The Christmas Conference for the Foundation of the General Anthroposophical Society 1923/24*, GA 260, Anthroposophic Press, 1990. pp. 270ff.

33. Rudolf Steiner, *Die Welträtsel und die Anthroposophie*. GA 54, 2nd ed. Dornach 1983, lecture of 16th November 1905. E.T. in typescript NSL 325, Rudolf Steiner Library, London.

34. GA 278 (see endnote 25), lecture of 23rd February, 1924.

35. Ibid.

36. GA 279 (see endnote 4), lecture of 25th June, 1924.

37. GA 277a (see endnote 18), p. 107.

38. GA 233a (see endnote 29), lecture of 12th January, 1924.

39. Ibid.

40. Rudolf Steiner, *Seelenübungen mit Wort- und Sinnbild-Meditationen. Seelenübungen, I, Übungen mit Wort- und Sinnbild-Meditationen zur methodischen Entwicklung höherer Erkenntniskräfte 1904 –1924*. GA 267, Dornach 1997, p. 212ff.

41. Rudolf Steiner, *Mythen und Sagen – Okkulte Zeichen und Symbole*. GA 101, 2nd ed. Dornach 1992, lecture of 26th December, 1907. N/T.

42. GA 267 (see endnote 40), p. 218.

43. GA 264 (see endnote 2), p. 181ff.

44. See Werner Barfod, *Tierkreisgesten und Menschenwesen, Ein Weg zu den Quellen der Eurythmie*. Dornach 1998. N/T.

45. Hildegard Bittorf, *Eurythmie*. Weissenseifen 1993.

46. GA 277a (see endnote 18), p. 38ff.

47. Rudolf Steiner, *Education for Special Needs*, GA 317, Rudolf Steiner Press, London, 1998, lecture of 5th July, 1924.

48. GA 279 (see endnote 4), lecture of 12th July, 1924 (with variations).

49. Werner Barfod, *"Ich denke die Rede"*. 2nd ed. Dornach 1996. N/T.

50. Florin Lowndes, *Enlivening the Chakra of the Heart*. Sophia Books / Rudolf Steiner Press, London, 1998.

51. GA 278 (see endnote 25), lecture of 23rd February, 1924.

52. GA 279 (see endnote 4), lecture of 11th July, 1924 (German ed. includes reproduction of the manuscript of the verse).

53. R. Steiner's formulation.

54. Ibid.

55. Rudolf Steiner, *Nordische und mitteleuropäische Geistimpulse*, GA 209, 2nd ed. Dornach 1982. Lecture of 23rd December, 1921, E.T. in typescript Z 389, Rudolf Steiner Library, London.

56. In *Mitteilungen aus der anthroposophischen Arbeit in Deutschland*, Stuttgart (Advent) 1952.

57. See Chapter 8, p. xx and GA 233a (see endnote 29), lecture of 12th January, 1924.

58. See Werner Barfod, *Die drei Urphänomene eurythmischen Bewegens*. 2nd ed. Dornach 1996. N/T.

59. See Rudolf Steiner's Notebook Entry of 4th August, 1922, in Rudolf Steiner, *Eurythmie. Die Offenbarung der sprechenden Seele*. GA 277, 2nd ed. Dornach 1980, p. 284. N/T.

60. See endnote 49.

61. Lecture of 7th October, 1914, in Rudolf Steiner, *Zeiten der Erwartung – Neue Formen der alten Schönheit aus der Welt des Geistes*, Dornach 1935, p. 20ff. (not yet published in the Complete Works). N/T.

62. Rudolf Steiner, *Festivals and their Meaning*, Rudolf Steiner Press, London, 1996. Lecture of 4th June, 1924.

63. In order to bring differentiation into this exercise, "the three archetypal phenomena of human movement" would be of value. These are not gone into here, however. See endnote 58.

64. GA 277a (see endnote 18), p. 107.

65. Ibid., p. 24.

66. Ibid., p. 36.

67. Ibid., p. 37.

68. For a detailed presentation on the theme, see *inter allia* Werner Barfod, *Die drei Urphänomene eurythmischen Bewegens*, 2nd ed. Dornach 1996.

69. For further details see the previous chapters of this book.

70. Rudolf Steiner, *Architecture as a Synthesis of the Arts*. GA 286. Rudolf Steiner Press, London, 1999, Lecture of 28th June, 1914,.

71. All of the eurythmy exercises, elements and forms here mentioned are assumed to be already known within the thematic context presented in: Annemarie Dubach, *The Basic Principles of Eurythmy*, Mercury Press, Spring Valley 1996, and in: Rudolf Steiner, *Die Entstehung*

und Entwickelung der Eurythmie. GA 277a (see endnote 18). Here one finds descriptions of all the prerequisite fundamentals.

72. Lecture of 9th January, 1915, in Rudolf Steiner, *Wege der geistigen Erkenntnis und der Erneuerung künstlerischer Weltanschauung.* GA 161, Dornach 1980. E.T. in MS in Rudolf Steiner Library, London.

73. GA 279 (see endnote 4), lecture of 24th June, 1924.

74. GA 279 (see endnote 4), lecture of 25th June, 1924.

75. GA 279 (see endnote 4), lecture of 26th August, 1923.

76. GA 279 (see endnote 4), lecture of 1st July, 1924.

77. GA 279 (see endnote 4), lecture of 25th June, 1924.

78. See endnote 21, lecture of 17th July, 1923.

79. See: Rudolf Steiner, *Entwürfe zu den Eurythmiefiguren.* GA K26, 2nd ed. Dornach 1984, and *Die Eurythmiefiguren von Rudolf Steiner,* painted by Annemarie Bäschlin. GA K26a, Dornach 1987. N/T.

80. GA 278 (see endnote 25), lecture of 21st February, 1924.

81. Regarding gnosis, see: Peter J. Carroll, *Liber Kaos – Das Psychonomikon,* Edition Ananael 1994.

82. Rudolf Steiner, *Twelve Moods,* Mercury Press, 1984.

83. Ibid., p. 9.

84. GA 277a (see endnote 18), p. 159f.

Notes

Notes

Notes

Notes

www.ingramcontent.com/pod-product-compliance
Lightning Source LLC
LaVergne TN
LVHW051752080426
835511LV00018B/3309